FINISH YOUR BOOK

Praise for *Finish Your Book*

"The author's passion definitely comes through from start to finish, offering both creative inspiration and practical advice for the writing journey."

Paula Wagner
Author, Career Coach

"There's a wealth of good suggestions in this book. One of the biggest takeaways for me was to have a comprehensive writing system."

Ivan Farber
Author, Podcaster, Speaker

"This book deals with every aspect of the writing process: blocks, procrastination, delays, interruptions, the whole nine yards. It makes me feel encouraged and empowered."

David Hern
Author, Playwright, Screenwriter, Actor

"You may be unfamiliar with methods of making writing a healthy habit, but you'll be more informed after reading this book."

Linton McClain
Author, High Performance Coach

"The quadrant grid in this book was incredibly valuable for me. It clearly laid out my options, showing why certain approaches might not work as well as others, and emphasized the importance of being part of a broader community."

Ryan Christopher Hicks
Travel Writer, Audiobook Expert

FINISH YOUR BOOK

PLUG INTO THE POWER OF A WRITING COMMUNITY AND GET IT DONE

LORRAINE HAATAIA, PH.D.

PROLIFIC WRITERS PRESS/PHOENIX, AZ

Prolific Writers Press
Phoenix, AZ
www.prolificwriters.life/press
press@prolificwriters.life

This publication is designed to provide accurate and authoritative information about the subject matter covered. It's sold with the understanding that the author and publisher are not engaged in rendering legal, intellectual property, accounting, medical, psychological, or other professional advice. If legal advice or other professional assistance is required, the services of a competent professional should be sought. The author and publisher, individually or corporately, do not accept any responsibility for any liabilities resulting from the actions of any parties involved.

Bulk ordering information: Volume pricing may be available for bulk orders placed by corporations, associations, writing groups, and other organizations. For details, contact the "Special Sales Department" of Prolific Writers Press at the address above.

FIRST EDITION

ISBN: 979-8-9910100-0-9 (e-book)
ISBN: 979-8-9910100-1-6 (paperback)

Cover design by Renée Chio
Editing and interior design by Tanya Brockett, Hallagen Ink

PROLIFIC
WRITERS
PRESS

This book is dedicated to you, my dear reader and fellow writer. May your dream of writing and finishing your book become a reality. I wrote this book for you with the hope that it guides and inspires you to share your writing journey.

Contents

Preface

This book isn't a traditional how-to guide. You've likely encountered countless tips about staying up late, waking up early, or writing 1,000 words a day—methods that work for some but may not resonate with you. Perhaps you've tried these approaches before or are seeking new strategies. Instead of offering a one-size-fits-all solution, this book provides a wealth of tips, resources, and encouragement from my writing life. It's not about doing it solo; it's about thriving within a supportive network. Unlike many other books on writing, this one emphasizes the power of collaboration and community. I share lessons from my writing journey and my experiences with various writing groups and individuals.

I wrote this book for one main reason: to encourage you, my fellow writer, to become part of a writing community. Most writers enjoy solitude, finding solace and creativity in those quiet moments alone. This is a natural and necessary part of the writing process. However, it's only one part. Another essential aspect is the teamwork involved in writing, publishing, and promoting your book. This teamwork begins the moment you start your book, and it continues throughout the entire journey.

Being part of a community of writers is the single greatest thing you can do to support your writing journey. I'm not just talking about a few friends who happen to live nearby. I'm referring to a writing community where you connect with dozens of writers from various backgrounds and genres. These fellow writers are there to support and encourage you, offering different perspectives and invaluable feedback.

If you're currently experiencing the value of being an active member of a writing community, you'll easily grasp the essence of this book. If not, join us at Prolific Writers Life, and you'll experience firsthand the value of being surrounded by a community of writers. Plugging into a writing community will open your eyes to the incredible support system available. However, as you and I well know, writers tend to be curious people. You might be interested in knowing why you should be part of a writing community when working on a book.

This book is a helpful guide to understanding the value of being in community with fellow writers. It explores different types of writing communities, ways writers gather, and how to build and develop your own writing system within these communities. Whether you're connecting with industry experts who are a few steps ahead of you or supporting writers who are just starting, everyone has something valuable to share. Newbie writers don't even know what questions they need to be asking, and authors who are working on their second, third, or fourth book still have much to learn about writing, publishing, and marketing a book. Wisdom and ideas flow freely when writers gather to discuss their books, their lives, and their writing journeys.

This book is not necessarily meant to be read from front to back, though doing so will provide you with a comprehensive understanding of the value of community. Feel free to jump around, scanning the subtitles and sections to find the information you need. I have structured it intentionally to serve as a guide, encouraging you every step of the way.

I have been a writer ever since I can remember. There's something about being around fellow writers, being around books, and being immersed in the world of words that feels like home. It's where I belong. As a fellow writer, I deeply care about your writing journey. I'd like to share with you why taking part in a writing community, especially when you're working on a book, is so vital to your success.

My writing journey has been shaped by the writers and experts I've met at conferences, critique groups, book festivals, and many other gatherings for writers. I gained ideas and knowledge from these events, but rarely felt a deep sense of belonging. Everything was too fleeting, and it was impossible to keep in touch with all the interesting people I met.

But once I started Prolific Writers Life, it really started to gel for me how transformational this kind of writing community can be for writers. Although I can't predict the future for you, I can tell you that I'm excited about the opportunities and connections you can make when you are part of a lively writing community. Whatever you do, don't write all on your own. Your writing journey will be so much more fulfilling when you share it with a community of fellow writers.

It's time for us to embark on this journey. From this moment on, you will see that you are not alone. A supportive writing community is waiting to welcome you and help you get your voice out to the world. Whether you're just getting started on your first book or you've been writing for many years, I assure you that your story is worth sharing, and your writing journey is worth commemorating with fellow writers.

CHAPTER 1

Why Do You Want to Write a Book?

Many people say they want to write a book, but either struggle to get started or stall shortly thereafter. I like to ask people, "Have you ever thought about writing a book?" It's a fun conversation starter, especially when someone shares a unique aspect of their life, whether it be tragic or triumphant. Perhaps they've achieved something that most people cannot or would not do. Or maybe their story revolves around a life experience that, while not extraordinary, resonates with many, like the loss of a loved one or another type of change that transformed their life. Regardless of the nature of their experience, it's how people handle it and how they go through the journey that makes the story compelling.

If you have a positive outlook, regardless of what happens to you, you're qualified to write a book. There are plenty of negative people who can benefit by learning from you.

When I meet good storytellers, I ask the same question: "Have you ever thought about writing a book?" Often, people say "yes," but then quickly rattle off a list of reasons why they can't start writing a book yet.

If you want to finish your book, your "why" must be stronger than your "why not."

Writers are compelled to share their thoughts and experiences through the written word. It's a unique calling. This shared passion is reason enough for writers to gather much like other interest groups, such as gardening clubs, photography clubs, or music groups. These are your peeps who share common interests, values, and pursuits. Each time you gather with writers, the collective knowledge of the group expands. When you participate in a writing mastermind (i.e., a community of authors and experts in the writing industry), the collective wisdom is much greater than any individual member.

The desire to write a book is deeply personal, but it becomes more meaningful when you share your ideas with others. Fellow writers offer motivation, support, shared learning, and a sense of camaraderie, enriching the writing journey for you and the community. As you progress with your project, fellow community members keep you grounded, reminding you of the purpose behind your book and the value it has to offer.

So, how can you get support from a writing community? First and foremost, they need to know what you're aiming for and why. And they need to know when you want to get there.

"Oh no!" you might be thinking. "Do we have to talk about accountability, deadlines, and all-out dedication to our projects? This feels like an attack on my creative process."

I know. I felt the same way for many years. I didn't want any authority to put deadlines or compulsory restrictions on my creativity. When I was working in academia and later in the corporate world, I wrote books, but I didn't publish them. After years of having university deans, business managers, executives, and other bosses directing my career, the last thing I wanted was for someone to oversee my creative life.

Outwitting the Devil

In his book *Outwitting the Devil*, Napoleon Hill explains how the "devil" manipulates people into a state of confusion. He confounds them with lots of meaningless options, making it difficult for people to have clarity on their purpose and direction. When you don't know where you want to go or why, you can take any road, and you'll always feel lost. You don't know how to make decisions. The best answer you can muster up is "maybe."

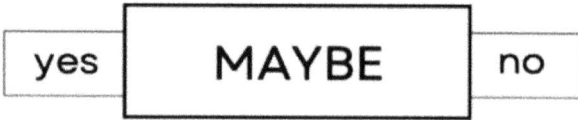

| yes | **MAYBE** | no |

It's great to know that you want to write a book, but it doesn't do you much good until you decide the purpose of your book and what target audience you want to reach. If you don't know what you're trying to accomplish, you don't know what to say "yes" or "no" to when you're deciding what should or shouldn't be included in your book. Should this or that be included? Maybe. It's nearly impossible to write a cohesive book when you're unsure of its purpose.

Hill forces the devil to disclose the solution: To escape this quandary, be decisive about what you want and devote yourself fully to the pursuit of your heart's desire, such as publishing a book on the specific title of _____ (fill in the blank) by the date of ____ (fill in the blank). Once you make your decision and know why it's important to you, you'll have the clarity to make informed choices about what belongs in your book.

Knowing your purpose provides clarity in all your decisions.

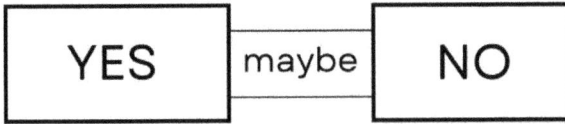

```
+-------------------+       +-------------------+
|                   | maybe |                   |
|       YES         |-------|        NO         |
|                   |       |                   |
+-------------------+       +-------------------+
```

When you know the purpose of your book, it's much easier to decide what belongs in the book and what doesn't. It's critical to establish your direction, voice, and perspective before you dive into writing your book. This is an essential step that enables you to be decisive, to know exactly what to say yes to, and what to say no to.

The Impact of Indecisiveness on Writing Progress

Indecision often results in people deferring their decision-making to others. Failing to take charge and make decisions in your own life results in yielding to the choices made by those around you. If you want to publish a book, you must take the lead and persevere to the end. According to Napoleon Hill, indecision is the villain that you need to evict from your life. You can take immediate action on this and start to get clear about what you want.

The Power of Knowing Your Why

Writing a book is a form of self-expression. You hope to make an impact and you have some expectation of achieving personal fulfillment. But what impact do you want for you and your readers? Your journey begins with a fundamental question: Why do you want to write this book? It's knowing that motivation deep inside of you that sparked you to embark on this journey in the first place.

Your Why is Your Guiding Light

Your why is the lighthouse that keeps you moving in the right direction. It shapes all your decisions and helps ensure that your efforts are focused and effective. Homing in on your why is the quintessential first step in any writing project.

Being part of a writing community can greatly assist you in clarifying your purpose and setting the direction for your writing journey. While choosing your initial "why" is essential, being open to adjustments throughout the project is equally important.

If you tend to be indecisive, writing a book can feel like a daunting challenge. As a writer, you're making a decision every time you choose to put a word on the page and every time you choose to delete a word. Given that most books consist of tens of thousands of words, this can be an intimidating process — enough to keep any indecisive writer from ever reaching the finish line. To make matters worse, you may have a critical editor voice in your mind who won't let up — she works overtime incessantly reminding you that things need to be improved, rewritten, revised once more, and then tweaked indefinitely. If you have a perfectionist editor who has taken up residence in your mind, it's time to tame her and welcome some positive friends from a supportive writing community into your life.

As a member of a writing community, you can get valuable insights into decision-making from fellow writers, authors, and industry experts. Ultimately, this can help you accelerate your progress and give you confidence about your chosen direction. This doesn't suggest that you should count on them to make decisions for you. The point is to gain deeper insight into your strengths and weaknesses when it comes to decision-making and practice the habit of being more decisive about the content and direction of your book.

Your "Why" Facilitates Decision-Making

Understanding your "why" helps you make decisions more quickly and effectively. Knowing the purpose of your book is essential because it guides every choice you make. Without a clear outcome in mind for your readers, it's difficult to decide what should or shouldn't be included in your book. Don't worry about getting it perfect on the first try — your "why" can evolve, and you can always make adjustments as needed.

Your Why Defines Your Niche

First-time authors often assert, "My book is for everyone." Seasoned authors are more realistic in their approach. They understand that their book has a specific audience. Being an active member in a writing community will help you sharpen your focus. Understanding why you're writing and what attracts readers helps you tailor your message to resonate with your audience. Each book has its unique readership. Knowing your why allows you to embrace your niche, be relevant within it, and make an impact.

Understanding your motivation for writing the book provides you with clarity, helps you identify relevant content, and pinpoints your target audience's needs. This insight serves as a guiding light, helping you make informed decisions and stay on the right path.

The Evolution of Your Vision

While defining your "why" at the outset of your project is crucial, keep in mind that your vision can evolve. It can shift as you go deeper into your writing project. When you begin writing a book, you get started, but you don't necessarily know where it's going to take you. Your vision may shift as your words begin to flow.

Perhaps you never considered monetizing your book. But through the process of writing, you realize that you can help people who are facing struggles you've overcome. Or maybe you only had plans to share your book with your family, but as you get deeper into the project, you grow in confidence. When fellow writers in your writing community are fascinated by your stories, they will naturally encourage you to publish.

Your response to audience insights may evolve as you progress on your project. Delving deeper, you'll likely grasp their needs, interests in your book, ways it can assist them, and potential interaction points. This evolving understanding may refine your desired outcomes. You might decide to add a book club section to the back of your book, launch a podcast, create a workbook to accompany your book, use the book to promote your business or a humanitarian project, or seek opportunities as a keynote speaker. Be open to what can come out as you're working on your book and sharing the journey with fellow writers.

If your book is already part of a larger plan, your writing community can provide valuable support. Discussing your aspirations within the community opens access to wisdom, experiences, and new connections. By initiating these discussions, you'll uncover a wealth of knowledge and insights from fellow members. Writers need readers once their book is out, but writers also need support from fellow writers before and after the book is out.

The Purpose-Driven Community

The journey of writing a book is much more than just putting words on paper. It begins by understanding your driving force — why are you writing this book? Once you determine the purpose of your book, share it with the community. This helps to keep you accountable and strengthens your resolve to complete it when distractions arise or doubt creeps in.

Not only can knowing your why help with accountability, but it also can be very empowering. Sharing your *why* with others in the community creates mutual support because they have visions for their books, and you can support and encourage them as well. When you share your purpose with others, it reminds them that they, too, need to keep their purpose top of mind. It has a positive ripple effect throughout the community.

Going through this mutually supportive and creative process together creates strong bonds over time. Because you're deeply immersed in the creative process together, you're well positioned to boost each other on your current writing project and manifest the broader scope — the writing life you desire.

The Influence of Your Words

I read a lot. I collect books. I crave books. When life gets busy, I read one or two books a month, and when I have the time, I often read (or listen to) one or two books a week. If I get just one great idea from a book, it is worth my time. Typically, I get dozens of good ideas from each book I read.

Writing a book isn't just something you put on your to-do list. It's a profound exercise and practice of churning knowledge, stories, and ideas, and releasing them into the world. Not only does the reader benefit from the transfer of knowledge, but the reader also spreads seedlings into the minds of people they touch. Books are the way that writers connect with their readers. It's the way they inspire change.

Words are a means of a timeless connection between writer and reader. Book pages have little value in and of themselves. The value comes through the intimate connection between the author and the reader. This is what resonates with your readers years later. It only takes one phrase, one idea, or one story to have a profound impact on someone's life. Your words can change the course of history. It might not be easy, but it's worth your time and effort to finish your book.

The Transformative Influence of a Writing Community

If you struggle with indecisiveness, a writing community can give you the backing needed to navigate challenges and make confident decisions. When immersed in a community of fellow writers, you're backed by a team of cheerleaders and impromptu coaches who want you to succeed. Fellow writers offer constructive feedback, which helps you gain a deeper understanding of your project in a way that is unattainable when you work alone.

Initially, your motivation for writing may seem straightforward—perhaps sharing a story, leaving a legacy, or addressing a personal trauma. However, engaging with a writing community exposes deeper layers of motivation. Discussions reveal unforeseen aspects of your purpose that contribute to self-understanding. This can enhance the depth of your book in ways you never considered. A book typically begins with an idea, and it ends with several themes running throughout.

The book you write on your own may satisfy your curiosity, but the book you write in community is more likely to address the interests and needs of many. Coworking in a writing community not only gives you access to support and guidance, but it also uncovers those hidden motivations and enriches the depth of your writing. Ultimately, the collaborative spirit of a writing community empowers you to transcend indecisiveness and create a book that resonates with a broader audience, fulfilling both your personal and collective aspirations as a writer.

What Message Do You Have for the World?

Reflect on the everlasting endurance of a book—a time capsule that extends beyond the life of you, the author. Books can outlive their creators, impacting lives far beyond their publication dates. As a writer, your unique calling and passion drive you to gather and share experiences. When you face challenges in writing your book or lose touch with your why, remember the extraordinary power embedded in your pages. Your book has the potential to impact lives long after you're gone. In writing for today's generations, you're also leaving a lasting message for future ones.

The transformative influence of a writing community cannot be overstated. Engaging in discussions and sharing your journey with fellow writers enriches the depth of your writing and empowers you to transcend indecisiveness. Remember the extraordinary power embedded in your pages. Your writing journey is not just about the destination; it's about the profound message you leave behind—a timeless testament to your passion, creativity, and unwavering commitment to sharing stories that change lives.

CHAPTER 2

What Does it Take to Finish Your Book?

From my childhood, I felt a call to write. My teachers encouraged me to pursue my writing talent, but it was a different story at home. Unfortunately, many writers lack support from their family and friends. My family had the best intentions, warning me to avoid lofty dreams and settle for something more practical, like becoming an engineer or accountant. If it weren't for those supportive teachers and librarians who lifted my creative spirit when I was in school, you wouldn't be reading this book.

Friends and family can offer some encouragement, but writers have a deeper understanding of the writing life. They understand the challenges you face. They know all about good writing days and bad ones. They know the feeling of losing traction. Fellow writers can help you get back on track, but they need to know what track you're on.

In addition to writing a book, have you considered other goals for your writing life? Do you want to publish a bestselling book? Do you want to build a coaching business around your book? Do you want to go on a virtual podcast tour to create awareness about your passion project? Do you want to turn your book into a movie? Knowing your goal is essential for both you and your fellow writers. It's helpful for your support team to know what "true north" means for you. When you're involved in a writing community, you get the support you need to imagine and take steps toward building the vision you have for your life as an author.

For your peers to support you, however, they need to know where you want to go. They're not here to judge you on your progress; they're here to help you stay on track and go at a pace that makes sense for you.

A coworking community of writers is a simple concept in which a group of writers work together in the same physical or virtual space. Coworkers perform tasks independently, but in the company of one another. Members benefit from collective knowledge, shared resources, and mutual encouragement. Surrounding yourself with fellow writers can help you overcome feelings of imperfection, self-doubt, isolation, or anything else that holds you back from writing. Not only does this benefit you in your writing journey, but it also benefits your overall well-being. Conquering common struggles together empowers you to overcome obstacles and emerge stronger. Being part of a coworking writing community, such as Prolific Writers Life, can enhance your creativity and productivity. Daily coworking sessions give you the chance to check in with fellow writers on your progress. Social interaction provides you with a supportive network and a boost in your overall well-being.

If you're working on your first book, you likely have many questions—from writing to publishing to marketing. If you try to do it all on your own, this journey can feel isolating, leaving you with unanswered questions and regrets about some of the decisions you make, but it doesn't have to be this way.

Trying to navigate your writer's journey alone can be a turbulent experience. I remember one of our Prolific Writers Life experts, Coach Linton McClain, emphasizing that "there's only one shortcut, and that's to have a team." That's exactly what a writing community does for you. It gives you a team of people who are cheering you on, mentoring you, and providing inspiration, knowledge, motivation, and accountability.

The Writer's Journey

The writer's life involves finding time for writing, deciding where to write (at home or elsewhere), and embracing many tasks that come with releasing a book into the world. It's a journey filled with questions, from the initial "How do I get started?" to "What should the title be?" to later questions about publishing and marketing options.

If you're used to writing in isolation, it's a fundamental shift in your thinking to become part of a writing community. But this shift can be one of the greatest decisions of your writing life. Many writers crave the opportunity to work in seclusion, free from interaction with the outside world. Although there will surely be times when you want solitude to go into deep focus on a project, know that this is but one facet of the writing process. If this is all you do as a writer, you're missing out on one of the most exhilarating aspects of writing — sharing the writing journey.

Successful writers know they need a team of supporters to bring their book to fruition. The natural process of a writing life involves real-world experiences: interaction with people, storytelling, and working with your editor, book cover designer, publisher, and others. These interactions are common and frequent for successful writers. Collaborating with fellow writers and industry experts provides the means to get answers to your questions and recharge your creative battery. The energetic power you get back through these connections is priceless. Companionship is the path to fulfillment in your writing life.

From Isolation to Collaboration in Writing

If you attended a public school or if you went to a college or university in the United States, you were brought up in a culture that isolates students and forces them to fend for themselves. Humans aren't like this, and schools shouldn't be like this either.

Aside from the occasional group project, most schools in the United States focus on testing individuals and assigning grades like A, B, C, D, and F. Team spirit is destroyed little by little, year after year, in academia. By the time students graduate high school, if they're lucky, they still have a desire to learn, read, and grow. Chances are, you graduated from high school without fully experiencing the many benefits of collaborating with writing companions, for example.

It's no surprise that many college students dread English classes that require independent reading, research, and writing. Incidentally, these are some of my favorite things to do. When I taught composition and writing courses in colleges and universities, I set aside conventional methods. I had students reading each other's essays, commenting on what they liked, and collaborating on ideas to develop their writing skills.

Many students came into my classes with their arms crossed and eyes rolling when I promised that they would love writing by the end of the semester. Within a few weeks, those same students came to class with growing confidence and an increasing appreciation for the written word. This was because they started to experience the powerful influence of writing companions.

Back when I taught, there weren't any online apps that rated professors, but when it came to sign up for next semester's classes, word spread among students. Students who took my classes recommended me to their fellow classmates. My classes filled fast, and I was often asked to add an additional class to handle the overflow.

If you're reading this and you happen to be one of the many students who took one of my classes, please reach out to me and let me know how you view writing today. For me, one of the most gut-wrenching parts of being a professor was saying goodbye to my students at the end of each semester, knowing that I may never see them again. One of the things I love most about Prolific Writers Life is that we have been forging lasting relationships ever since we launched in January 2020.

What You Say to Yourself Matters

You never have to be alone on your writing journey. Contrary to what many writers believe, you can do some of your best writing in the company of fellow writers. Being part of a writing community allows you to tap into a flow of consciousness with others who are also on a mission to share their words with the world. By mingling with experts in the industry, you position yourself in a place where fresh ideas are flowing. Imagine working alone in a closet with no air flow. Not only does this stifle your imagination, but this dark seclusion also encourages your fearful and critical inner voices to prod and alienate you. How is it possible to be in the best state of mind when you're working in seclusion with little to no encouragement?

When you work in isolation, you're at risk of being jinxed by critical self-talk. When you work in the company of fellow writers, you gain the courage and know-how to evict those critical inner voices.

My friend Ivan Farber, author of *Conversations: How to Manage Your Business Relationships One Conversation at a Time*, increased my awareness of how to have better conversations. Moreover, he shared his story of how Shad Helmstetter's book, *What to Say When You Talk to Your Self*, had a tremendous positive impact on his life. Ivan writes about conversations with others, but also believes that the conversations you have with yourself are of paramount importance. Book recommendations can be very helpful and powerful—this is yet another benefit of being in a writer's community.

Picture yourself in a writing community where words and ideas are flowing—words of encouragement, and words of support—how does that feel? Imagine how much more appealing such a workspace can be. There will indeed be times when you want to write alone, but you never have to be alone as a writer. When you're in a supportive writing community, you increase your odds of reaching your writing potential. Don't risk the chance that your dark inner voices speak up and hold you back. Join a writing community where you can surround yourself with like-minded friends who have your best interests in mind.

When you position yourself in a writing culture, you become unstoppable. Let me make this perfectly clear. You do not have to go it alone as a writer. You'll be much better off when you work in the company of fellow writers.

The Buzz of Assembly

Let's go back in time for a moment. I went to a big high school that had hundreds of students. Your high school might have been bigger or smaller. Do you remember those school assemblies when all the students and teachers gathered in the gymnasium to enjoy the band's music, listen to announcements, and engage with speakers? Can you conjure up the buzz of energy that radiated from students who were freed from the confines of their classrooms to enjoy an hour or more of togetherness and connection?

This is the kind of group energy you tap into when you get together with fellow writers. I can't explain how much more motivated and inspired you'll be when you're part of a writing community. It's something you need to experience in order to fully appreciate it.

The Lifeline for Your Writing Soul

Many people rely on external sources — like prescriptions, medical procedures, social services, or prayers — hoping they will be saved without realizing the immense internal power they possess. By aligning your thoughts, energy, and spirit, you can tap into this power to accomplish big goals, such as writing a book. Your stories, however, originate from deep inside. Even if you were to hire a ghostwriter, you would still need to articulate your book concept. The work of the writer is to draw words from within and share them with the world. Writers do indeed need ongoing connections with their readers and with fellow writers, but ultimately, your book's message originates deep inside you.

Why I Write

When I was in middle school, I transferred from a private Catholic school to a public school, where I experienced less discipline. In Catholic school, obedience was strictly enforced, but public school introduced me to kids with more freedom and different attitudes. Around this time, I was grounded for something, most likely for talking back to my mom, and banned from watching TV for a week or two. Although I enjoyed watching cartoons like *Bugs Bunny/Road Runner Show, The Jetsons, The Flintstones,* and a few programs such as *The Brady Bunch*, being blocked from TV opened me up to a world of imagination through books and writing. Realizing that I could never be grounded from reading or writing, I immersed myself in these activities. My parents couldn't distinguish between my school reading and writing from what I did for pleasure, so I had unlimited access to both. This grounding from TV turned out to be one of the best things that ever happened to me, as it sparked a lifelong passion for reading and writing, opening up a whole new world for me. That grounding was decades ago. But to this day, I still don't watch TV.

Fast forward a few years from that grounding, one of my older brothers, Bobby, drowned in the St. Johns River in Jacksonville, Florida, at the age of 25. It was the summer before the start of my sophomore year in high school. It's hard enough being a high school student without the additional turbulence of losing a sibling. This tragedy set off an emotional storm inside of me, leaving me overwhelmed and enraged. I turned inward to try to sort out my emotions, seeking solace in the written word. I had already been writing, but this loss intensified my need to write even more. It became a sanctuary where I could freely express my rage, grief, and confusion. How could anyone else possibly understand the depths of what I was going through? Writing became my lifeline, a way to navigate through the pain and find some semblance of peace. If only he had been swimming with friends instead of alone, he might still be with us today. But there was nothing I could do to change the reality of what happened. Writing has a healing power, and I have personally experienced it many times. Here's a poem I wrote about my brother that was published in the *American Poetry Anthology* in 1982:

When I Wake Up

I talked to you all night long
In my dreams
When I woke up
I closed my eyes and asked you to come back
But you didn't
Now I dream about scary monsters
When I wake up
I close my eyes and ask you to come back
But you don't.

Several teachers encouraged me to write and go on to college to continue studying so that I could pursue a career related to writing. In some ways, these teachers were a lifeline to my writing soul. They saw my talent with writing, and they encouraged me to follow my dream.

In my junior and senior years of high school, I was the editor-in-chief of the high school newspaper. I enjoyed highlighting stories of what was going on at our campus. Back then, we had to type up the stories using a typesetting machine that set the type into justified columns. The text was printed on crisp, silky photo paper. I used scissors to cut the columns into pieces and puzzled them together on the layout boards, using a wax-like glue to secure the columns. It was both an art and a science, satisfying on multiple levels. The process was deeply gratifying—not just the art of storytelling, but also the connection with people in the school, the creative joy of cutting, pasting, and laying out the words, images, and advertisements. It brought together so many fun elements, and I was thrilled with the look and feel of the final product. But the most rewarding part was seeing my fellow classmates reading the paper.

Although I'm not making newspapers these days, I'm still working with words in ways that connect with my life purpose. When your writing practice connects with your deep calling, you know you're in the right place. This is your lifeline—the connection between your soul and the written word. For journalists, it flows from them in the form of news that informs the public. For poets, it flows through the stanzas, helping people to meditate on new perspectives. For comedians, the lifeline flows through the jokes and ignites when people laugh. For authors, the lifeline flows through the book, into the minds and lives of the readers, plus there's a ripple effect that goes out to everyone that all of these writers reach.

Expert Guides

My husband and I enjoy traveling abroad. We've traveled to dozens of countries together. Most of the time, we plan the trip on our own. We look at reviews from people who have traveled to this particular location. Getting advice from people who have been there is very helpful. They write notes and reviews along the way. I enjoy books that include maps and highlights of the local attractions. Expert guides warn you about risky areas and the people, places, and situations you should avoid. The recommended attractions vary from book to book and from one travel review site to another. Everyone has different interests and perspectives, so when you're looking at reviews, it's helpful to read ones from a variety of people. It's quite common for one attraction to have a broad range of ratings, including ones (from people who did not have a good experience) to fives (from people who had a great experience at the attraction).

In October 2012, my husband and I traveled to Indonesia for what we thought was going to be a leisurely vacation. When we arrived by taxi at the Ritz-Carlton in Jakarta, we encountered unexpected security measures. My husband and I, as well as the taxi driver, all had to get out of the taxi. Security guards took all our luggage, including my handbag. We watched in surprise as armed security guards used mirrors and wands to look under the taxi and comb through everything inside the taxi and its trunk. The guards used wands to screen us and police dogs to sniff us before we were okayed to go into the lobby. Despite our research and preparation, we were unaware of the current unrest until we were on site. The concierge advised us to stay on the hotel grounds for safety. He warned us to be extremely cautious about walking around the city.

Of course, there's much more to this story, but this experience underscores the importance of having expert guidance in the moment. When you're writing a book, having access to fellow writers, authors, and industry experts is crucial. You can benefit by reading books about writing that were published in recent years, but nothing is as valuable as getting advice from locals when you're on your journey. Just as a local guide provides timely insights during travel, being immersed in a community of writers offers essential support and real-time advice during the writing process.

This is what it's like when you work with experts: You might get conflicting advice, but by sticking with it and engaging with a variety of experts, you'll discover what works most of the time and, more importantly, what works best for you. With one guide, you gain one perspective; with multiple guides, you can blend their advice, gaining a deeper understanding and making better decisions that resonate with your unique journey. Every writer's path is different, which is why the expert guidance found in a writing community is an essential element of a successful writing journey.

Beware of Grifters and Scams

Some writers, eager to get their passion projects off the ground, make hasty decisions without considering the risks and possible consequences. Over the years, I've met many writers who have fallen for various scams. They don't readily share their stories with just anyone. They must have some level of trust to open up and reveal these enraging or embarrassing experiences.

For example, I've known several writers who have tried to save money by hiring people overseas to edit or format their book. There's nothing wrong with hiring someone overseas, but you need to ensure you're dealing with someone trustworthy and with the skills to do the work. If you hire someone without reviewing their qualifications, you might face issues if they lack the necessary expertise or reliability.

Beware of websites where you can't find the names, pictures, or contact information of the people in charge. Be cautious of people who have no website and run their business through social media. Look out for inconsistencies in their business name across their social platforms. Be wary of unsolicited emails or direct messages from their social media platforms. And be cautious of any links they send you in direct messages or emails.

Watch out for people who charge thousands of dollars to help you write and publish your book in ninety days. Even if you manage to get through this hasty process, the quality of your book will likely suffer. Watch out for wolves who prey on sheep. Some people make big promises, ask for big bucks, and set you up for disappointment, or worse yet, they disappear with your money. And there's little you can do about it.

Instead of taking a risk with someone you know nothing about, you're better off reaching out to fellow members in a writing community and following up on references from people they trust. You might spend a bit more money, but you'll get the product or service you paid for. Your writing community is the perfect place to bounce around ideas and ask for recommendations. If you're seeking a writing coach or book doula, for example, be sure to ask for at least three references and follow up with them. Making good decisions about the people you work with and avoiding grifters is reason enough to join a writing community.

Beyond Knowing: Practicing

It's easy to gain knowledge about how to write, publish, or market a book, but you go to a whole new level when you actually go through each of the steps with your own book. You can read a book or watch a video about book writing, book editing, or how to find an agent, but you don't master these things on your first go around. You're much better off being in a community where you have access to authors and experts in the writing industry and benefit from their knowledge and wisdom. However, just because an expert has knowledge doesn't mean they know what's right for you. When you work with a variety of seasoned experts, you have the benefit of the collective wisdom they've earned after years of experience in the industry. You grow in discernment as you put their advice into practice and make decisions about your book.

If you were given the choice to have your book edited at a discount by an English teacher who graduated from college last year or have your book edited at a higher cost by a professional editor who has edited hundreds of books, many of them bestsellers, who would you choose? Although you might be tempted to go with the English teacher who's offering you a bargain price on editing, the overall quality of your book will turn out better with a seasoned editor.

The English teacher and the editor have more knowledge of the English language than the average person, but the professional editor has a deep understanding of the book industry, what needs to be edited, how a book should be formatted, and much more.

There's no shortcut to attain this wisdom. It can only be earned through years of experience in the industry.

As you invest more time in a writing community, you gain knowledge that continues to deepen into wisdom in your particular areas of interest. If you plan to write more than one book, you'll benefit tremendously by growing your skills in the following areas:

- Reading and having a basic understanding of the workings of your genre
- Discovering the best publishing path for you
- Developing strategies for book marketing and building your author platform

All of these will help you expand your knowledge in areas that are important to writing, publishing, and marketing your book. The best way to get started is to engage with a writing community and take small (and sometimes even giant) steps toward your goals each and every day. Together, we can achieve our writing dreams.

"Get Used to the Feeling of Finishing Things"

A few years ago, in one of our Prolific Writers Life advisory board meetings, we were discussing strategies to help writers get their books done. One of our advisory board members, Linton McClain, shared a nugget of wisdom as he often did. He said that writers need to "get used to the feeling of finishing things." Once you do, it becomes addictive; the sense of accomplishment and the dopamine rush from completing each project strengthens your motivation to tackle the next one.

Imagine yourself holding your finished book. What do you envision doing with it? Do you picture yourself going on podcasts and talking about your book? Do you imagine yourself doing a reading from your book at a local bookstore? How will your life be different after your book comes out? If you have questions about how to finish your book and what life might look like after your book comes out, read on. A writing community is the ideal place for you to discover how to get started, how to maintain your momentum, and, ultimately, finish your book.

Welcome to this journey. I invite you to be part of the Prolific Writers Life community, where we gather to support, encourage, and lift each other up. With support from fellow writers, you can finish your book and have fun doing it.

By now, I hope you have better understanding as to why you want to write your book and what it really takes to finish it. Now, let's take a look at your role as a unique writer, shaped by your life experiences, beliefs, values, and feelings. Your authenticity is the very thing that makes you attractive.

CHAPTER 3

Your Authenticity is Attractive

How many times have you heard the phrase, "nobody's perfect"? While this is universally acknowledged, it can be the very mindset that slows down your writing process. We know we have flaws, but we don't necessarily want other people to know certain flaws that trigger negative memories. We do our best to write around our vulnerabilities.

When I actively participated in comedy improv, I was fascinated with Rule #1: Always agree and say "yes" to everything. If a fellow improv partner says, "You're stupid," you must agree and add to the story. "Yes, my brother always told me I was stupid, too." Unlike comedians who often use their flaws as material for humor, you may not want to flaunt your imperfections, write about them, or admit to them. Most writers prefer to present themselves in a more polished or idealized manner. However, what holds true in your life will undoubtedly show up in your writing life. Ironically, the more authentic you are with yourself and your readers, the more likely they are to connect with you and become loyal fans.

If you want to finish your book, recognize that your work extends beyond mere storytelling — it requires you to confront your self-perceived flaws and plow through them with sentences and paragraphs. As you compose and edit paragraphs and chapters, you can gain insight into how you perceive and cope with these aspects of yourself, not only during the writing process but also in certain life situations. It's nearly impossible to write without revealing some of what you see as your strengths and weaknesses, even if others might view them differently. The act of writing can be a transformative journey for anyone who completes a book.

Our authenticity gets hidden behind layers over the years. My parents told me what I shouldn't do. You shouldn't be a writer. My peers, teachers, siblings, church leaders, friends, cousins, nuns, aunts, bullies, grandparents, priests, neighbors, professors, police, actors, preachers, news broadcasters, spouses, bosses, and others told me what I should and should not do. As the years passed, I collected layer upon layer of things I shouldn't do in certain circumstances. I can't speak out in school the way I would at home, and I must behave differently in church than I do at work. I can drive fast on the freeway until a highway patrol officer pulls me over. I can joke freely with my friends or siblings, but I need to be more reserved with parents and teachers. To blend in, I allowed my authentic self to be covered by countless onion-like layers that obscure who I am. I've been walking around for years, collecting layers of conformity that shield my authentic self, the true "I am." Am I the only one, or can you relate to this?

Every now and then, I come across someone whose presence lights up any space they enter. Their aura shines brightly, unburdened by the weight of those onion-like layers. They carry a vivid, magnetic energy that people recognize on a subconscious level. They know who they are, where they came from, and where they're going. This confidence makes them naturally attractive to others, who are drawn to their strength, wisdom, and enthusiasm. They not only freely acknowledge their own mistakes but also recognize their shortcomings without letting them hold them back. They are confident in who they are and, in their purpose, sometimes even laughing at their flaws. People like this are magnetic and inspiring, with an aura that radiates their true selves.

Open Up and Be Vulnerable: Authenticity is Funny

One of the fundamental principles of comedy is making fun of yourself. By pointing the finger at yourself rather than others, you avoid coming across as threatening. This approach often triggers laughter because it allows the audience to relate and feel less self-conscious. You create a connection with them when they see themselves in your experiences and feelings.

There is immense power in acknowledging your flaws. When you allow yourself to be vulnerable, it resonates with others. It's an invitation to connect and laugh together about common foibles. Countless times, I've witnessed speakers joke about their traumatic or dramatic life experiences on stage. Inevitably, one or more audience members flock to them afterward with questions and words of appreciation and encouragement.

Laughter is a universal form of therapy that can help relieve tension, stress, and worry. Even when readers' experiences don't exactly mirror yours, they can relate to your pain and challenges. This applies to both fiction and nonfiction writing. Authenticity has widespread appeal.

Stick around fellow writers who are open about their strengths and weaknesses. You'll find that those who have a light-hearted approach to their peculiarities also have a better outlook on life and people. Not only can this be a healing process for your personal and writing life, but it's also fun and rewarding to overcome perfection tendencies together.

Flaws are Rooted in Perception

I love the classic answer to this aphorism: Question: What's the difference between a weed and a wildflower? Answer: A judgment.

If a plant shows up somewhere that someone doesn't want it to be, then they judge it to be a weed. Some consider dandelion to be a weed, while others treasure it as a source of herbal medicinal tea with many health benefits. Same plant...different perspectives. The dandelion isn't necessarily a flaw in someone's front lawn. It's labeled a flaw in the lawn from the perspective of the beholder.

You may be enthralled with a book by your favorite author, while many others would never consider buying the book, and even if they received it as a gift, they would soon pluck it out of their bookshelf and donate it. There's nothing inherently wrong with the book. A book that's a page-turner for one person goes into the Did Not Finish category for someone else.

Most Flaws are Invisible

One summer when I was in grade school, I took a camping trip from Pennsylvania to Florida with one of my cousins and his grandparents. Our destination was their Florida home, complete with a big sandy yard and a swimming pool. One evening after dark, my cousin and I were having fun skinny dipping and chasing each other around the moonlit yard. We were innocent kids enjoying our summer break from the confines of school. The house had awning windows, which were hinged at the top and opened outward from the bottom using a crank. As my cousin and I were running around the yard, I took a turn close to the house and pierced my forehead on the corner of one of the awning windows that was open. Blood gushed from my forehead down into my eyes and onto my hands. Our fun that evening ended as I ran inside crying for help.

For the next few weeks, I had a big scab about an inch down from my hairline, right in the middle of my forehead. People kept asking me, "What happened?" But to me, it felt like they were asking, "What's wrong with you?"

After some time, the scab finally healed and fell off. Eventually, the red mark turned into a faint, slanted white line scar that, to this day, is still there. I'm probably the only one who knows it's there, and the only time I see it is when I use a magnifying mirror to apply makeup. Ironically, this scar is above my third eye — a close reminder that our scars can become accent marks of wisdom and character.

The reason I'm telling you this story is to remind you that most people will never notice your flaws or your physical or emotional scars, even if you're reminded of them every day. We all have subconscious records of our scars and shortcomings that inadvertently affect our confidence when it comes to writing and publishing a book. Will it be good enough? Will someone attack me or my book once it's out there?

Flaws Can Be Charming

Some of the most powerful speeches I've ever seen on stage have been delivered by authors who confronted seemingly insurmountable challenges. If you have lived through personal traumas or faced significant challenges, it's common to feel flawed or broken. You might feel as if you don't stand up to the other, more perfect people around you. Whether it's struggling

47

with self-esteem issues, dealing with the aftermath of addiction or divorce, or coping with a mental or physical disability, at some point, we all feel as if our spirits have been tested or even attacked.

What's crucial to remember is that the life experiences that leave you with scars are the very things that create an intimate connection between you and your reader. Your "flaws" make you relatable to people who connect with you because of them.

When you're among fellow writers, it's like looking into a mirror. They understand the challenge of writing about experiences they'd rather not revisit but feel compelled to share, whether in fiction or nonfiction form.

Writers know best how to encourage fellow writers to release the grip of perfectionism and share their imperfect lives. No matter how you tell your story, the important point is that your story gets told. It's not a good use of your time to procrastinate or hold back. This tendency is stifling not only to your writing, but also to your life and everyone who can benefit from what you have to share.

I know writers who keep lists of character traits, including flaws, scars, weaknesses, strengths, and quirks, because these are essential ingredients for character building. Fiction writers know that characters must have both virtues and vices to be relatable. For example, a character might have flaws like stubbornness or impatience. They might have scars from a past trauma or weaknesses such as a fear of failure. Their strengths could include resilience or empathy. Additionally, they might have unique quirks, like humming when they're nervous, showing up late for meetings, or preferring to go barefoot whenever possible.

Imperfection is a form of beauty. When you're honest about something that has happened in your life, people are drawn to you because you have the courage to share your story. Consider this: most people (some estimate as many as 95%) do not have the desire or courage to share their stories with the world through a book. Your willingness to share your story, flaws and all, demonstrates a remarkable openness, which is alluring.

This is Not a Competition

You are not in competition with other writers. Your goal is to tell your story and get your book out to as many people as possible. No one can write your story, so there is no one to compete with. Support and learn from your friends who have published successfully — and they'll gladly support you when your book launches. If you want to compete with somebody, it should be yourself. Set up metrics for your writing pace, and eventually your promotions and sales. Then strive to break your own records.

Your Scars Give You Credibility

Over the years, I've met many authors who have written books about areas of their lives where they have gone through near-death experiences, addiction, molestation, incarceration, terrifying battlefield experiences, and much worse. They've experienced shame, embarrassment, trauma, humiliation, depression, and many other difficult emotions. Other writers seem to go through life unscathed, yet they still have sensations of shortcomings. When writers decide to share their stories, they also choose to relive these experiences repeatedly as they write, process, and edit their stories. Whether they lost a spouse, job, or a limb, they've decided to expose their deepest pains in exchange for something bigger.

Symptoms of Perfectionism

Subconsciously, a perfectionist knows she isn't perfect, but she strives to achieve perfection in particular areas of her life. Her desktop is stacked with papers, while the drawers inside the desk are neatly organized with rubber bands in boxes separate from the paper clips and pens, for example. The box of paper clips provides a sense of order in chaos. How do you know if you're a perfectionist? Here are some ways that perfectionism manifests in the lives of writers.

Going Overboard with Writing, Researching, or Editing

Have you ever written a story thousands of words long, only to have someone tell you that you could cut more than half the words? Or have you traveled to foreign countries to do research because you felt it was necessary only to abandon the project altogether? When you share stories like this in a writing community, you'll meet fellow writers who can relate. This is a chance to gain awareness of your life tendencies and, through your writing, begin to escape the claws of perfectionism that cause you to overedit your manuscript or do much more research than necessary.

Self-Doubt

Do you feel you must live up to an unattainable standard of perfection? Throughout our lives, we adopt many beliefs—some are factual; others are fictional. In the process of writing, do questions like this plague your thoughts:

- Is it acceptable for me to tell this story? Yes.
- Do I have the right to tell my story? Yes.
- Are my language skills good enough to write? Yes.
- Could I be shunned by family members or friends for telling the truth? Perhaps.

If you had the inspiration to start a story, that is the only confirmation you need to move forward. When self-doubt creeps into your consciousness, there's a good chance that your inner critic is attempting to under-mine your confidence and creative process. Don't let this jinx you. Surrounding yourself with fellow writers is a way to ward off self-doubt.

Conversing with other writers who grapple with similar struggles is empowering. You may find that you have more confidence or respect for your peers than you have for yourself. Their insecurities and chal-lenges are invisible to you, while your own are magnified. Insecurities tend to ease up in the process of building friendships. As friendships grow, you come to realize that friends and readers focus on the value of your story. Most people don't even notice what you recognize as your insecurities or imperfections.

Being an active member in a writer's community can help to provide the encouragement you need to settle your insecurities and move on with writing. You have every right to share your story and how it impacted your life.

Too Much Talk, Not Enough Writing

Another symptom of perfectionism is the fear of sharing your writing with others. Some writers are willing to talk on and on about the ideas they plan to include in their book, but they're unwilling to share a passage from what they've written. This may keep them from joining critique groups, or if they do, they spend a lot of time justifying the state of their manuscript. Or, they talk over people who are offering suggestions. In some cases, they may repeatedly bring the same chapter to a critique group in an attempt to perfect it.

Seeking input from readers is valuable, and sharing excerpts with them cultivates comfort in letting others in on your writing process, even when your chapters aren't "ready." Chances are, your work is better than you give yourself credit for.

It's beneficial to receive feedback during the writing process. Whether you're participating in an open mic, attending a critique group, or sharing a few chapters with an accountability partner, it's good to get in the habit of sharing what you're writing. Ultimately, the purpose of writing is to share your pages with readers who are interested in what you have to offer.

Editing Too Soon

Another symptom of perfectionism is obsessing over every sentence or every word and spending too much time correcting grammar in your early draft. None of this matters in your early draft; it will all be cleaned up in the end. The most important thing is to get the main storyline down on paper. Later, after you've gone through the revision process, when you feel your manuscript is ready, send it to your beta readers, and finally to an editor to do the fine-tuning. If you find yourself over-editing or overwriting, allow your peers to help you get through the perfectionism.

Stops and Starts on Multiple Projects

If you're juggling several writing projects at a time, it can be difficult to complete any one of them. It's normal to sprout new ideas regularly. Expect this. You're a writer. When you participate in a writing community, fellow writers recognize this and help to provide accountability to focus, to stick to one major writing project at a time until you finish it. You cannot succeed as a writer if you're constantly sprouting new ideas without completing any of them.

Procrastination

Procrastination is often a symptom of perfectionism. You put things off because you're too concerned about getting it right. Seeing other writers in your writing community moving forward on their projects will encourage you to make progress on yours. By interacting with fellow writers, you'll get updates on their progress and, therefore, feel more inclined to let them know how your writing project is progressing. You'll recognize that they, too, are imperfect, and they make mistakes and struggle with their lives and stories, too. Everyone faces challenges that can be used as excuses to procrastinate. But together, the collective progress elevates the entire community. Seek out writing communities where you can grow and share your struggles. Find and embrace a nurturing environment that keeps you moving forward and provides a space for your authentic voice to flourish.

Fear of Publishing

Another symptom of perfectionism, the fear of publishing, impacts your book's visibility. Perhaps you're not afraid of writing the book or sharing your story with a few people in a critique group or an open mic. But when it comes to actually publishing the book, you find reasons not to put it out there. Something holds you back. That resistance might be the fear of rejection. Or you may fear your book won't sell as many copies as you want, or you worry about how your friends and family will react to it. The key thing to know here is that all writers, authors, and public figures, in general, will face criticism; not everybody will like your story. That's okay because you didn't write it for *everybody*. Your book doesn't have to be a perfect fit for everyone; some people will like it, and some might not, but no one benefits if you don't publish it.

The Value of Your Perspective

Some writers experience paralyzing doubt after they discover that similar books have already been written.

There isn't one perfect way to share a story. There are many ways you can convey a message, and there's a very good chance that your way will resonate with a certain niche audience. Remember, your perspective is genuinely unique. Although others may have gone through similar experiences, they haven't had your specific experience. In fact, some of your experiences might be completely foreign to them. We all benefit by writing down our stories and sharing them with others. Stories radiate like campfires, attracting people to circle around to share in the laughter, tears, and lessons.

Another writer could be writing a romance novel with beach scenes, but it's not your story. This is why writing your book from your perspective is so valuable—it's unlike anyone else's. Don't try to copy others who have written similar books. Be authentic and true to your own story.

By sharing your stories, you give others insights into their relationships and lives. You add the greatest value when you're true to yourself—when you fearlessly share from your heart. Stay active in a writing community. Not only will it give you practice in sharing your perspective, but you'll also grow your confidence and learn valuable lessons from fellow members.

You're the Perfect Author for Your Book

As you spend time with fellow writers, you'll come to realize that readers in your target audience will appreciate your book. Those outside your niche simply won't connect in the same way. Your book isn't meant for everyone. If you feel the desire to write a book, chances are you're the ideal author. You don't need to second-guess your qualifications. Clearly, you can't do the impossible. If you know nothing about tunneling, it would be silly to attempt to write a book about how downtown tunnel systems are constructed.

When I was working on my dissertation in graduate school, I immersed myself in a sea of books, articles, and research papers to come up with a unique message to add to the body of academic knowledge. If you don't have experience or knowledge in a certain topic, be ready to dive into thorough research so your book feels authentic and believable to your readers.

Comparable Books are Allies

When it comes to selling your book, one of the initial steps authors often take, especially when writing a query letter, is to identify comparable books. What are comparables? This involves searching for books that share similarities with yours. Assuming you find books that are similar to yours, your task is to explain how your book is different from other books on similar topics (i.e., offers a new perspective). Even if you plan to self-publish your book and you're not required to get comparables, it's good to be aware of other books like yours.

At this point, some writers panic and think that since there are already other books like this out there, there's no point in writing another one. This is yet another reason why writers need support from a community.

Regardless of how many other books are out there, remember that you have a unique perspective to offer. It's essential to shift your perspective and realize that you are not in competition with these books or the authors of these books. In fact, many readers who are interested in this subject are likely to be interested in your book as well.

Feedback: Your Path to Growth

Some of your most valuable lessons as a writer come from receiving feedback, whether it be in the form of criticism, edits, or even rejection. Feedback is a powerful tool for gaining insight into other people's perspectives and enhancing your own growth as a writer. Not only is it important for you to be authentic, but you also want authentic feedback on your writing.

The key is to approach feedback with an open mind and a willingness to learn. Rather than dwelling on the negatives, view feedback as an opportunity to improve your work. Feedback can provide valuable insights to enhance your storytelling skills and deepen your connection with your audience.

Wouldn't you rather have people's authentic feedback on your book and get their honest review prior to it being published, when you still have the opportunity to change it? This is much more valuable to you than them just telling you, "Oh, I like it."

A writing community can provide support and guidance through the feedback process. By surrounding yourself with fellow writers who are invested in your success, you can gain valuable insights, encouragement, and constructive criticism and take your writing to the next level.

Embracing feedback, both positive and negative, is a fundamental aspect of the writing journey. It allows you to refine your work before it reaches its final form. It's a way to ensure that your book resonates with readers as you intended. It requires vulnerability and humility, but the lessons you learn and the growth you experience are worthwhile. Invite feedback with open arms. It's a means of growth. Each insight brings you one step closer to creating a masterpiece.

Focus on Process and Progress, not Perfection

Perfectionism is a trap you want to avoid if at all possible. It can have a negative impact on many areas of your life, including your writing life. If adult influencers such as parents or teachers told you that you weren't good enough in even one area of your life, it could put you in a perpetual and detrimental cycle of trying to reach unattainable goals. Your fellow writers can help you gain awareness and evict the inner critic. Instead of focusing on the perfection of the end product—your book—strive to improve your writing process to continuously put out better and better chapters. Perfectionism that stifles your production is self-defeating. Continuous improvement that produces results, such as captivating book chapters, is healthy.

Writing a book can be like putting together a puzzle. You begin by finding all the pieces with a straight edge, making the outline of the picture. From there, you go piece by piece, filling in all the details until you have a clear image of what you're creating.

Avoid focusing on the whole product you're creating, and instead focus on the outcome of actually writing the words, paragraphs, sentences, and chapter titles. Imagine how much progress you're making, and focus on the process of writing instead of allowing yourself to become overwhelmed with the whole scope of the project. Ultimately, you get through the whole process one chapter at a time.

Authenticity is undeniably attractive, both in life and in writing. As writers, we hold the power to connect with readers on a profound level by embracing our imperfections and vulnerabilities. By confronting our flaws head-on and sharing our authentic selves with the world, we invite others to join us on a path that changes lives. Remember, you are the best person to represent your story, and being genuine is the most compelling way to present your message to the world. Embrace feedback with an open mind, focus on your process and progress, and trust in the unique value of your perspective. In doing so, you'll not only strengthen your writing but also forge deeper connections with your audience. Let your authenticity shine through and watch as your story resonates with readers in ways you never imagined possible.

CHAPTER 4

Mastering the Art of Consistency

Curtis Chin, the author of *Everything I Learned, I Learned in a Chinese Restaurant,* grew up working in his family's business. Imagine sitting in a Chinese restaurant, with the clatter of plates, the buzz of conversation, and music playing in the background. Curtis learned to work through the chaos, balancing his schoolwork and the demands of the family business. While trying to do his homework, he also had to take customer orders and phone calls and help out wherever else he was needed. This created a whirlwind of activity that required him to shift his focus with lightning speed. Here, he honed a skill that would later prove valuable in his writing journey — the ability to seamlessly transition from one task to another and to concentrate regardless of what was going on around him.

As he toggled between completing his assignments and tending to restaurant duties, he developed a knack for diving back into his homework without missing a beat. While his upbringing may be unique, the challenge of maintaining consistency in writing is a familiar topic to writers.

What does it take to master consistency and stay focused and productive through life's distractions? Let's look at some strategies to maintain consistency in your writing.

Prioritize Your Health and Well-Being

Maintaining good health is crucial for nurturing your creativity and sustaining your writing journey. While it's easy to get caught up in the excitement of writing, neglecting your physical, mental, and spiritual well-being can hinder your productivity and creativity. Just as a mother cares for her child, an author often dedicates herself to nurturing her book, sometimes sacrificing sleep and personal needs to ensure its success.

Though occasional late-night writing may be tolerable, making it a habit can take a toll on your health and overall productivity. Unless the night shift is part of your usual writing schedule, it's wise to avoid staying up late and sacrificing sleep to write. With proper planning and support from your writing community, you can develop strategies to minimize the need for late-night work sessions.

Establish a writing routine that prioritizes your health and well-being. If you spend long hours in front of a computer screen, be sure to take regular breaks to rest your eyes and stretch your body. Every hour, step away from the screen for a few minutes—look out a window or, even better, step outside and focus on something in the distance. Take this time to stretch your neck, shoulders, and legs. You'll find that you're much more productive if you take the time to relax, recharge, and hydrate throughout the day.

Being part of a writing community can provide valuable support and guidance in maintaining your health and well-being. Through discussions with fellow writers, you can exchange tips and strategies for staying healthy and energized throughout your writing process. By prioritizing your health, you not only enhance your creativity and productivity but also ensure that you can enjoy fulfilling and sustainable writing habits for years to come.

Set Clear Writing Goals

Setting goals with deadlines is incredibly empowering. It gives you a clear sense of direction, purpose, and urgency. The primary objective is to structure your creative process, ensuring that your efforts are channeled toward achieving your desired outcome, especially when it comes to a big goal such as completing a book. Being part of a writing community allows you to share your goals, opening the door to valuable feedback and mutual accountability among fellow members.

Fellow writers are among the most essential companions in your journey. They offer valuable insights and unwavering encouragement, helping you maintain your course even when unexpected life events inevitably occur, putting your milestones or deadlines at risk.

Hone Your Habits

Over the past several decades, I've crossed paths with a vast number of writers. Many dream of getting away for a week or two to concentrate on finishing their book. In reality, very few authors write their books on getaways. The majority of authors succeed at completing their books because they've established good habits.

Practicing good writing habits is the key to tapping into your creativity and making progress on your book. It's all about embracing discipline and maintaining consistency in your daily writing routine. Instead of making excuses, make progress each day. Every moment you dedicate to your book is a step towards realizing your dream of finishing your book. While life may present its challenges, it's important to approach them with determination and resilience.

One powerful way to stay on track with your writing goals is by being part of a writing community. Surrounding yourself with fellow writers helps to keep you on track. It's a place where you can engage in discussions, share experiences, and learn new strategies for maintaining consistency in your writing habits. Within a writing community, you can inspire and motivate each other to overcome obstacles and stay committed to finishing your book. Whether your goal is to write 1,000 words a day or one chapter a month, it's crucial to establish habits and milestones that support your writing goals.

Fun First, Consistency Follows

Developing effective writing habits is key to completing a book. It's tempting to explore the various writing habits of successful authors in depth, but instead of focusing on habits, consider a different approach. Let's explore one of the most essential elements in the writing process—enjoyment.

When you genuinely enjoy the act of writing and find yourself making steady progress on your book, you're building good habits with ease. The joy you get from the process cultivates consistency. As you will learn from fellow writers, the goal isn't to force yourself to adhere to rigid schedules or follow strict rules. What's more important is that you find pleasure in the act of creation.

When one of our Prolific Writers Life members, David Hern, was working on his book, *How Not to Make it in Hollywood*, I was working on this book, *Finish Your Book*. At the same time, Ryan was hosting our Words Count writing sessions. He was in the middle of a 500-day writing marathon, counting down to his plan to graduate with his double-major master's degree, quit his job, sell his house, his car, and everything he owned, and move to Brazil. Ryan would start each session by saying, "It must be Monday." This was our cue to have some fun conversation as we checked in on our progress and shared what we were going to work on that day. Thanks to this routine, we all had fun, supported each other, and made progress on our goals.

If you find yourself stuck and unable to move forward with your book, figure out what's going on. Perhaps you're not enjoying the writing process as much as you could be. This realization presents an opportunity to explore what aspects of writing you find most enjoyable and how you can incorporate more of them into your routine.

When you find fulfillment in every phase of your writing process — from drafting to editing — it becomes easier to establish habits that support your progress. Enjoying the process naturally leads to a more consistent and productive writing routine. Whether it's working in the company of fellow writers, reading passages aloud at open mics, or experimenting with different writing environments, cultivating a sense of enjoyment will naturally lead to the development of positive writing habits. I like to print out my manuscript and read it outside on my patio, for example. It's easier to imagine my book as a book when I'm reading it on paper. To me, it's important to read my book in different contexts, outside of my office, to experience it in different environments as my readers would. Ultimately, embracing the joy of writing and editing is not only essential for completing your book but also for sustaining your passion for writing in the long run.

Establish a Consistent Writing Routine

Routines are a sequence of habits performed in a pattern that you repeat regularly. They're commonly formed without much thought. You form routines organically based on a series of activities you perform that help you maintain order in your daily life.

When establishing a writing routine, you prepare your mind, body, and spirit for your writing session. A set routine provides a mental cue that it's time to transition into creative mode. Writing routines consist of an infinite combination of possibilities, limited only by the creative people who come up with them.

Being part of a writing community can be instrumental in helping you establish and adhere to a writing routine, particularly if you engage in regularly scheduled online writing sessions. At Prolific Writers Life, we offer Words Count writing sessions. In these writing sessions, you write alongside fellow writers. These work sessions provide structure, accountability, and check-ins to form good writing habits and formulate writing routines that work for you.

I often prepare a cup of herbal tea or make a smoothie before settling down to write. The sound of the electric kettle at home or the hiss of the teapot in my RV serves as a welcome cue. It helps me stay hydrated, plus it adds a sense of tranquility to my writing process. We open our Words Count writing sessions with a five-minute check-in. We write for twenty minutes and then do another five-minute check-in. Then we write for twenty-five minutes and do a final five-minute check-in. Often, we linger on in conversation beyond the scheduled hour. This routine gives everyone a chance to vent, meet newcomers, ask for advice, and announce our tasks at hand. When you write with fellow writers, you're surrounded by people who understand your challenges and can help you solve them in the moment, allowing you to quickly get back into the writing process and enjoy it without feeling stuck or alone.

Establish Routines that Support Your Writing Sessions

Routines often involve a series of habits that are performed in succession. Whether you're writing at home or somewhere else, it's helpful to have routines that can get you in the right state of mind. It might be something as simple as hanging a "I'm writing. Do not disturb" sign on your door, putting on a headset to listen to your writing playlist, or turning off the Wi-Fi on your laptop.

I often cross my legs yoga style in a comfortable chair. I like to review where I am in the writing process and catch up with what chapter I'm working on. I also like to have my outline handy, so I can refer to it as I write.

If you find that your writing sessions aren't as fruitful as you'd like, it's helpful to be part of a writing community where you can talk with fellow writers to see what routines they've established in their writing lives. If you get just one good idea to add to your routine, it can have a long-lasting impact on your writing productivity.

Sometimes, routines that seem unrelated to writing can still affect your creative flow. It's only when we step back and observe carefully that we realize how even small habits can influence our writing life. There were times in my professional life when I had longer fingernails and toenails that were painted shades of red or pink. It seemed like the thing to do to fit in with my Florida family and friends who flashed their latest manicures and pedicures, wearing nothing more than little bikinis and flip-flops at the pool or beach. When I look back, I wonder why I ever fell into this routine that I didn't appreciate or enjoy, not to mention the toxic exposure to nail polish and nail polish removers. I abandoned this routine many years ago.

One of my routines as a writer involves a manicure, a pedicure, and trimming my cats' nails. When I write, I prefer to have short nails so I can type fast. I usually begin with a detox bath, soaking my hands and feet to clean and soften my nails. I have a nail trim kit that includes a quality set of fingernail clippers, toenail clippers, a glass nail file, and a stainless-steel nail file. I prefer to do this on a weekend when I have a little extra time and don't feel rushed. I like to go out on my back patio where I can enjoy the outdoors. As I'm trimming my toenails, I take deep breaths and appreciate that my feet and legs have supported me through countless walks and hikes, not only in the US but also in dozens of other countries.

As I'm trimming my fingernails, I feel gratitude for my arms, my hands, and fingers. And I'm grateful that I have a laptop and various other tech devices that support my writing life. Plus, I'm extra blessed with a techy husband who keeps them all updated, backed up, and running smoothly.

When my cats see me trimming my nails, they know what's coming—they're next. Sometimes they'll lie down nearby, waiting for their turn. This whole process of taking a bath and trimming my nails and my cats' nails is one that you might not consider to be related to writing. I do, however, because I know when my nails are short, I type faster.

At Prolific Writers Life, we discuss all aspects of our lives, including our pets. When fellow member David Hern found out I could trim my cats' nails, he admitted he was jealous. Then Paula Wagner chimed in, saying she wished she could trim her cats' nails as well, but they won't let her. She said she spends more money on her cats' manicures than on her own. If you're looking for one more reason to join a writing community, come for the laughs — whether it's about your pets or other quirks of the writing life.

Practice Fundamental Writing Skills

When novice writers think about essential writing skills, the first thing that might come to mind is grammar. While grammar is important, there's much more to learn and practice. Here are just a few of many fundamental writing skills:

- Audience awareness
- Transitions
- Paragraph structure
- Genre specifics
- Tense and voice

Don't panic. You don't have to learn everything all at once, and you don't have to learn everything before you publish a book. You can and should hire an editor to polish your ideas and improve your manuscript. Editors love doing this sort of work. Readers don't. When readers can't determine what you're trying to say, they'll ding you on reviews. That's why every writer needs a professional editor.

If you're interested, take time out to review basic writing rules and principles. If not, allow a bit more time to participate in a writing critique group or share your book with alpha and beta readers. If you lack basic writing skills, you might pay a bit more for editing, but don't let this stop you from finishing your book.

I have a bachelor's degree in English and French and a master's in Teaching English as a Second Language. Plus, I was a professor for quite a few years. Trust me when I say that you do not need to go back to college and get a degree in English to improve your writing skills. In fact, very few college courses are geared toward writing books. There are many other ways you can learn on your own or get assistance from others.

The first thing you can do, you guessed it, is join a writing community where you can get guidance from authors and experts in the industry who know you and can give recommendations that suit your specific needs and learning style. The better you know people, the more well-suited they'll be to give advice that will work best for you. What else can you do?

Read widely. Read a variety of books, essays, articles, and poetry. Note that I'm suggesting reading. You can also listen to audiobooks and pick up fundamental writing skills, but reading helps you internalize correct grammar and sentence structure. Anything else?

Download a writing software tool. Several applications give you real-time feedback on your documents. Seek advice from members of your writing community for tips on when to use and not use these tools. What else can you do?

Browse through writing guides, style guides, and grammar books. You don't have to read them cover to cover. Instead, treat them as reference guides and read sections as necessary, focusing on what aligns with your current needs. There are many online tools to help with grammar as well. I could continue with suggestions, but again, the best place to ask for advice is in a writing community where you can get suggestions from people who better comprehend your current context and circumstances.

Read In and Out of Your Book's Genre

If you love to write, you probably already love to read, so you might not need this reminder. But it is important to remember that reading is fundamental to becoming a good writer. Many people read in only a few genres. It's natural to gravitate toward one or two favorite genres, but as a writer, it's beneficial to explore books and articles outside of your genre. Not only will it help to enrich your creativity, but it also expands your world of possibilities.

In a writing community, it's inevitable that people exchange book recommendations. You'll often hear a fellow member say, "Oh, I just finished reading this," or "That was a great book," or "Have you read such-and-such book?" You get to chat about books and open new doors in your literary world.

Acquiring the habit of reading in different writing styles will give you new perspectives that will inevitably enhance your work. If you love book clubs, you'll love being part of a writing community where you can compare notes on all sorts of books.

Believe in Your Intrinsic Ability

Years ago, a friend invited me to participate in a week-long survival camp on Whistler Mountain. Amidst the various challenges we faced, one lesson stood out — the importance of integrity, both with others and with ourselves. Survival school taught me that being true to our word is not just about showing up on time or fulfilling commitments to others. It's also about honoring the promises we make to ourselves.

At the survival camp, we learned the significance of external accountability through teamwork and shared responsibility. If we promised to be there for a teammate or to catch them if they fell backward, we followed through without hesitation. Some people were terrified to participate in activities that tested our fears of height, darkness, fire, falling, and even attacks, not to mention camping out in the company of spiders, carpenter ants, mosquitoes, bees, and wildlife. Some people dropped out because they got injured or couldn't handle it. It wasn't just about meeting external expectations; it was about building trust and reliability within our team.

However, what resonated most with me was the realization that our integrity with ourselves is equally vital. Even without external deadlines or obligations, the promises we make to ourselves are just as important. Whether it's setting personal writing milestones or committing to self-improvement goals, honoring these promises builds confidence and self-trust.

Being part of a writing community reinforces this principle of accountability until it becomes second nature. By establishing strong writing habits and staying true to our word, both externally and internally, we pave the way for success and become prolific writers in our own right. So, remember to believe in your intrinsic ability and hold yourself accountable to the promises you make, both to others and to yourself.

Engage In a Writing Community

You don't have to write your book alone. One of the best things you can do is join a writing community and show up. As you may have heard, "showing up is half the battle." A writing community can give you the support system you need to keep going, considering everything else that's going on in your life. Within a writing community, you discover all sorts of strategies, insights, and perspectives that fellow writers have tried. Experimenting with new strategies helps you grow as a writer. When you become part of a writing community, you position yourself within a support network designed specifically for writers. It's where you can share your experiences, ask for advice, and appreciate the small wins.

When you're surrounded by this encouragement and guidance and the shared experience of fellow writers, you can propel forward so much faster than if you were working on your own. Taking part in a writing community can completely transform your writing journey into a rewarding adventure.

Celebrate Milestones and Successes

When you track and recognize the milestones you achieve along your writing journey, you're more likely to keep going. Whether you have just finished the first draft of a chapter or hit a word count target for your book, it's noteworthy. These are accomplishments, and they deserve recognition.

As Aron Ralston illustrates in his book *Between a Rock and a Hard Place*, and the ensuing 2010 movie *127 Hours* based on his 2004 autobiography, you should not go hiking on your own. In this extraordinary survival story, Ralston relays the perils of embarking on a solo hike and the horrifying tale of what he had to do to save his life.

Likewise, it's not wise to venture out on a book-writing journey on your own. You're much better off when accompanied by friends who want to join you. Share your good news with your writing community. They'll understand and share in your excitement. Even a brief discussion of your writing achievements brings joy to everyone and reaffirms your commitment to your goals. Support and encouragement from fellow writers can be a big motivator that keeps you moving forward.

You don't write a book in a year. You write it paragraph by paragraph, and chapter by chapter, one day at a time. Consistently showing up for your book and your community is one of the best things you can do towards finishing your book. The next big topic to address is how you go about writing your book. What is your writing system?

CHAPTER 5

Designing Your Writing System

During an author's event in Phoenix, Arizona, I had the pleasure of sitting next to a doctor who also happened to be an author. We talked about his recently published book, and he eagerly shared many ideas he had for future books. When I asked him which one he wanted to start next, he said, "None of them." I was surprised at his response, but he quickly continued, telling me about his profound aversion to writing his first book. He said it was a torturous ordeal, and he never wanted to go through it again.

It was disheartening to witness someone with so much knowledge and so many great ideas be defeated by the daunting process of writing another book. This encounter reminded me of one of the most crucial aspects of the writing journey — ensuring that your process is enjoyable and manageable.

Writing should be a rewarding endeavor, one that you eagerly return to, and never a burdensome task. It's important for you to discover a writing approach that resonates with you, as there are countless methods to explore beyond the one he found so dreadful.

If you have been working on a book, you have a writing system. You may not be conscious of what it is. In fact, you probably don't think about it much at all. You've come up with ways to go about your writing, and the next day, you do the same thing again. It's not until you start looking at your writing system that you can figure out what it is and then determine if it's working for you. Chances are, it has much room for improvement.

What is a Writing System?

Your writing system consists of everything that's involved in your writing life. It includes the tools you use, such as the software programs and the research tools, as well as the way you collect, store, and retrieve information. Your system also includes when you write, where you write, how you write, and what habits and routines drive your writing behavior. Your system also includes asking for feedback from beta readers or writing groups, and participating in a writing community. All of these elements, and more, make up your writing system.

Right now, you most likely have two different writing systems. The first system is what you would describe if someone asked you about it. This is what you perceive as being true for you now. The second is your real system, which really happens when writing. It's nearly impossible for us to consciously access all that goes on in our minds throughout the writing process. Let's call this the all-knowing, omniscient perspective on your system. It includes how you collect, process, and assimilate your ideas before they're ever written. It's that mysterious process of transferring ideas into words on a page.

Gaining Awareness of Your Writing System

You gain awareness of your writing system when you get involved in a writing community and compare notes with fellow writers. Listening to what's happening in the lives of other writers causes you to reflect and notice what you do relative to what other writers are doing.

Your writing system is your vehicle for recording your ideas into some sort of format where you can share them with the world. Just as cars have motors with all sorts of moving parts, so too do the inner workings of your mind. Only the omniscient, the all-knowing one, could track and trace all the bits and pieces in motion as your thoughts are transformed into words. The words mysteriously move from your thoughts onto the page and then eventually out to the world in the form of a book, for example.

I learned a number of important lessons about my writing system while working on this book. My writing flows better when I type rather than when I dictate. Either way works, but I get different results. When I dictate, I tend to get a higher word count and more ideas, but afterwards it requires much more editing and organizing than if I just type it in the first place. You have to test these things to figure out what works best for you. And it really helps to share these findings with fellow writers. By verbalizing it to fellow writers, you'll surely get relevant comments and feedback.

In Prolific Writers Life events and work sessions, we sometimes talk about the software and applications we're using, but this stuff is constantly changing, and it can be beneficial to experiment with new tools.

Otherwise, you're simply stuck doing things the way you've always been doing them, just because.

I chose to use a particular financial management software application to manage writing expenses based on a recommendation from an accountant. After paying a high monthly subscription rate for over two years, one of our members, Liza Olmsted, recommended another tool. Shortly thereafter, we made the switch to the new software, and this saved us a lot of money! Joining a writing community can indeed spawn financial rewards. If I hadn't been in that conversation in the community that day, I might have spent hundreds more dollars unnecessarily over the upcoming years.

These cherished colleagues and coworkers can open up a world of opportunities for you. I know a few writers who thumb type their books on their phone. This seems like a grueling process to me, but it works for a young father who can work on his book while also keeping a close eye on his toddlers at home. Another writer I know who thumb-typed his book was in his sixties. He didn't own a computer, and he didn't want to get one, but he did want to write a book. One of the best things you can do to improve your writing system is to spend time with fellow writers and openly discuss your writing process. Get around fellow writers as often as you can.

Romanticizing the Author's Life

In high school English class, I made up my mind that I wanted to be a writer. When I learned about Hemingway's life of hanging out in Paris cafes with fellow writers, I knew I wanted this life. When I learned about his home in tropical Key West, where he went to write surrounded by his many cats, this life sounded so appealing that I was willing to do whatever it took to have this lifestyle. Back then, the writing life seemed so simple. I now know that there's much more to living a writer's life than chatting with fellow writers at a Paris café and having a writing desk set up in a tropical home. The flight to Paris is long, the jet lag is tiring, and the job of cleaning up cat litter from multiple cats stinks. Yet I still desire this writing life — savoring casual chats with writers and writing from the comfort of home with my cats.

What is the setting for your ideal writing life?

- Farmhouse in the countryside with picturesque rolling hills
- Historic European flat on a cobblestone street
- Car-free life in a big city loft within walking distance of restaurants and shops
- Jet-setting to explore new countries

- Minimalist Zen retreat garden home near miles of wooded walking trails
- A recreational vehicle that you can park wherever your wanderlust takes you

After making several vision boards about my dream writing life, I have personal experience with how powerful they can be. Before the age of thirty, I had lived in both France and Florida. And I have since had the opportunity to experience all of my dream settings described in the above list. Since then, I have also lived in China, California, Washington, Oregon, Arizona, and traveled to dozens of countries. You can make a vision board alone or in the company of friends, but I have found it more effective to share this experience with enthusiastic friends. Once you get clear about how, when, where, and why you want to write, you are one giant step closer to making your vision a reality.

You might be at a place in your life where you're perfectly happy with where you write, but you'd like to create a wish list to spice up your writing life:

- Go on a writing retreat
- Build a shed in your backyard as your dedicated writing space

- Adopt a dog as a writing and walking companion
- Cut back on your work hours to free up more time to write

WARNING: If you think small about your literary pursuits, you'll get small results. Don't be afraid to think big when it comes to your writing life. Your higher consciousness has a magical way of delivering what you expect.

Sharing your writing life dreams out loud with fellow writers makes it easier to take small steps every day to move closer to your goal. When you visualize what you want, you're able to recognize when you're presented with the right opportunities you need to jump on. I encourage you to make a vision board and share it with fellow writers. Hold that vision in your mind and roll up your sleeves. It's time to get to work on the details of your writing system.

Set Up a Method to Capture Fleeting Ideas

The ability to capture fleeting ideas is one of the most essential habits for a writer. How many times have you had a brilliant idea, sure that you would remember it, only to find out that just a few minutes later, you lost that great thought? Regardless of whether you use a pen and notebook, an app on your mobile device, or index cards, it's important to create a system that works for you.

I've carried a pencil and paper with me ever since I can remember. I imagine it started in kindergarten when I carried a backpack between home and school. To this day, I still carry a pen and a small notebook or index cards with me wherever I go. I also have note-taking apps to capture fleeting ideas. I've tried a variety of them. Each of them has its own strengths and weaknesses. The key, regardless of your chosen tool, lies in mastering the habit of capturing ideas in the moment. This one habit can provide you with an endless supply of writing prompts. Each idea is like a gold nugget in a treasure chest.

Do you have a reliable system for capturing that next great idea in the moment and later retrieving it as part of your writing process?

Join a writing community such as Prolific Writers Life to tap into a treasure trove of writing insights. Fellow writers are a wellspring of wisdom, offering techniques to capture fleeting ideas and insights to enhance every step of your writing process.

List Making: A Key to Organizing Your Creativity

Author Keiko O'Leary recommends keeping a compliments list. In her book *Your Writing Matters*, she devotes an entire chapter to this concept, outlining the method and advantages of keeping such a list. She recommends keeping your list in one place. It has more impact that way. Whenever self-doubt creeps in, you can refer to your compliments list and be reminded of the admirable qualities others see in you and your work.

This is just a starting point. When it comes to list making, there are endless possibilities, such as lists of writing prompts, plot twists, character names, writing achievements, and favorite words. Rather than trying to remember where you put notes, it's much easier to keep like with like. This is the value of a list.

The types of lists you keep can vary based on your writing goals. Here are a few examples:

- Research Sources: Books, articles, websites, or experts for specific projects.
- Settings: Detailed descriptions and information about various story settings.

- Blog Articles: Ideas, works in progress, and published blog posts.
- Submission Tracker: Where you've submitted your work with dates and responses.
- Promotion Ideas: Strategies for promoting your book, blogs, or other content.

Lists are a terrific tool for managing fleeting thoughts. Regardless of whether the ideas relate to your writing, keeping lists helps assure you that you're capturing your fleeting thoughts. Putting a note on a list frees up your mind and allows you to get back to writing.

You might not consider housekeeping a relevant list for writers, but it is for me. I keep a list of house-keeping chores that can be done in between writing sprints. My list of housekeeping chores has dozens of items on it, but here are a few examples:

- Start a load of laundry
- Clean out the cat litter
- Load the dishwasher
- Clean the glass on my desktop

Before stepping away from my desk after a writing sprint, I sometimes give myself a thought prompt. With the current chapter fresh in my mind, I work through an idea while I'm doing a house chore. This approach allows me to make progress on my writing while I check off other tasks. Plus, it gives my eyes a break from the computer.

As you share your lists with fellow writers, you'll undoubtedly develop ideas for new lists or ways to enhance your existing lists.

The Writer's Escape

As writers, much of our work happens in our minds, where we escape the world to rewrite it on our terms. In theory, we're not bound by cultural rules—we're free to change them as we go. Writing is both an escape and a return. We enter our minds to find what we want to share, then come back to decide what we're ready to reveal. If we stay aware, we can embrace this cycle and connect with fellow writers on a similar journey.

This is the life of a writer. We channel thoughts. We jot them down. We move ideas around. We remove stories and replace them with different ones.

Some writers stack other habits with writing, such as drugs or alcohol, to enhance their escape experience. Drinking excessive amounts of coffee can cause headaches, and drinking excessive amounts of alcohol can cause hangovers. In his book *On Writing*, Stephen King shares his story of his drug and alcohol addiction and the fact that he barely remembers writing his novel *Cujo*. Headaches and hangovers are not the norm for most writers. It just so happens that some percentage of the population is prone to addictions, and some of them happen to be writers. Habits often come in pairs, so be cautious about your beverage choices when you're writing. Choose wisely.

Many writers write simply because they want to escape their past or present life. The point of the writing is to escape, not to share with the world. Journaling is a legitimate system for escaping the world and jotting down ideas that don't get judged or ridiculed. The act of opening up a journal is the entry into an escape hatch wherein you can connect with your higher consciousness through your written words.

Writers who create stories or books but never go through the process of publishing them are essentially journaling. While the writer escapes from the world in the process, the words also escape the possibility of providing value to others. Finally, the writer avoids what she possibly fears the most—criticism from readers. Although the words never reach readers, this too is a writing system, albeit broken from the perspective of those who favor publishing their works.

Is your current writing system working as you would like? If not, find a writing community as soon as possible. Here you will be able to gain awareness of your system, make decisions about what you might want to improve, and then practice what it takes to make your system work in such a way that you get the results you want. In the company of fellow writers and authors, you are much more likely to be encouraged to finish your book.

Your Personal Writing Space

When it comes to real estate, you've probably heard that choosing the right property is all about "location, location, location." The same is true when you're settling on a place to write. It's all about location, location, location. When going to college and grad school, I often lived in small apartments or homes with roommates. I rarely had the luxury of having much more than a desk and a bed in my room, with little space to set up bookcases or spread out my writing projects.

Even if all you have is a laptop, a notebook, books, and pens, it's important to create space for these tools in your life and home. There were times when I had to stow them away after each use due to space constraints or house rules, which made it harder to resume my work. This disrupted my creative flow, preventing me from easily diving back in whenever inspiration struck.

Some people, including writers, perceive that the only thing a writer needs to be effective is a computer or a notebook and a pen. Indeed, some writers are much more minimalistic than others. If you can hammer out bestsellers with nothing more than a laptop, kudos to you. It simplifies your writing life. For most writers, it's not quite that simple.

Many writers have creative minds with eyes that wander and soak in their surroundings. What's in and around your writing location can greatly impact your productivity. I'm visually oriented, so I find it helpful to have inspirational things around me when writing. My office is decorated in black and white: black bookcases on one wall, white bookcases behind me, a black desk with a glass top, and black filing cabinets. I appreciate the simplicity of not having a color scheme in my office. It's black and white, mirroring the printed page. This way, the colorful books stand out against the monochromatic background of the bookcases. Nearly every day, I attend virtual meetings with Prolific Writers Life community members. They see the white bookcases behind me, but I see much more.

Above my desk hangs a large magnetic glass write/wipe board adorned with colorful images that serve as inspiration and remind me of my purpose. While I don't rely on it for writing, I enjoy its presence and the gentle subconscious nudge it provides. It's an ever-changing vision board for my writing life.

Having your writing space set up at all times is like having an entrance into your stream of consciousness, like having a stream in your backyard, continuously flowing and inviting you to dip your toes in whenever you please. This constant flow remains present in your mind, offering the flexibility to contribute thoughts or draw from it at any moment.

Often, when I'm doing household chores like washing dishes or hanging laundry outside, I'll get an idea. I appreciate the convenience of being able to walk into my office and dip into that stream of creativity, jotting down a note in my journal or adding a thought in my latest manuscript, seamlessly adding to my flow of thoughts.

Establishing your own writing space is an important component of developing a productive and fulfilling writing routine. Whether it's a minimalist setup with just a laptop or a notebook, or a carefully curated environment adorned with inspirational décor, having a designated space dedicated to writing fosters focus, creativity, and consistency. Regardless of the size and style of your writing space, what matters most is that it serves as a sanctuary where you can immerse yourself in writing and perhaps even draw inspiration from your surroundings. By prioritizing a space and environment conducive to your work style and preferences, not only will you enjoy the writing process more, but you'll also be more productive.

Finally, when you surround yourself in a community of writers, you'll get all sorts of good ideas about managing your writing environment(s) both at home and away from home.

Your Psychic Writing Space

While writing this book, I felt the stress of the looming deadline to complete the manuscript. My husband and I decided to head up to Sedona for a long weekend. I knew that at some point during the weekend, I wanted to soak in some of the healing power of Sedona: the mountains, the energy, and the people. I wasn't sure exactly what I needed; I only knew that I wanted to be led by my inner guide. On Saturday, during an afternoon break from writing, I considered several possibilities. I finally decided to go to a healing center with a high rating. I was greeted by Nathan "Nate" Townley, author of *Awakening Within the System*. The fact that he was an author gave me immediate confirmation that I was in the right place.

I scheduled the next available reading, which was with Heather Green of Teal Healing. As I was waiting for my appointment, I looked up Heather's website and found out that she, too, was an author. She is the author of *For the Love of Horses: An Animal Communicator's Guide to Helping Our Horses and Healing Our Lives.* Then I knew for sure I was in the right place. What are the odds of connecting with two authors like this? Nothing is an accident.

I spent a delightful hour with Heather. She asked great questions to find out what I was hoping to accomplish in that day's session. Her intuition was spot-on. One of the many interesting things she mentioned is that I need a lot of psychic space around me to write. Again, I was assured that she had tremendous intuitive powers. The whole session went on like this, with her affirming my current strengths and challenges with writing and publishing this book. The second part of the session with her involved clearing the energies and blocks holding me back for quite some time. Again, I felt she addressed the major issues blocking my energy.

Finally, she gave me some recommendations for expanding my energy and strength as I modified my life and made more space for this book. She closed with a few final suggestions. She encouraged me to keep citrine and rose quartz around when writing or meditating. Coincidentally, I pointed out that I was wearing rose quartz in one of my bracelets.

As one of my parting questions, I asked her what spirit animals I might count on as a writer. Without hesitation, she mentioned that a horse is a terrific spirit animal for writers. She also said that cats were great spirit animals for writers. Ironically, when I first launched Prolific Writers Life, I wanted our mascot to be a zebra. I played with this idea for about the first year after launching the writing community.

I thought the zebra was a perfect spirit animal for a writing community. It's black and white, like lines on a page. Plus, zebras are wild. They're free spirits that are difficult to tame and ride. This is the energy I want to instill in writers — to keep their wild nature and not allow anyone to saddle, bridle, tame, censor, or dismay them. I still have some zebras tucked away at home. However, for many reasons, my advisory board advised me to back off on this effort of making the zebra the mascot for our community. After returning home from Sedona, I put the zebras back on display in my office.

I don't doubt the advice I got from the advisory board. I think it was the right decision at the time. The pencil peace sign logo for Prolific Writers Life has no relation whatsoever with a zebra. One of the best parts about being a writer is that even if I edit the zebra out of our community brand, I can recycle the zebra idea into a story, blog post, or book like I'm doing now. Through the written word, I can keep the zebra alive in my mind and life.

By the time Heather and I were done, I felt like I had just come out of a deep massage that loosened up all my muscles. It felt like that, but even better because it also felt like a huge weight was lifted off my spirit, my back, and my shoulders.

I wish I could tell you that Nate and Heather were active members of a writing community when they wrote their books, but this isn't the case. When I told them about Prolific Writers Life and how much a writing community can benefit writers, they responded positively, recounting all the difficulties they faced in publishing their books independently. It opened their eyes to how much a writing community could have helped to facilitate the process.

I'm not sharing this story with you to suggest that you need to run out and schedule an appointment with an alternative practitioner. I'm sharing it with you to let you know that you never know what kinds of stories you might hear from fellow writers when you're a member of a writing community. Some of you may toss this idea to the wayside for now. Others might want to schedule an intuitive reading.

Regardless of your feelings about energy healers, it's important for you to know that there are many modalities you can tap into that can help you improve your writing system.

The Best Time to Write

Before I get into the common advice about finding your best time to write, I'd like to talk about journalists — people who have tight deadlines to pound out news stories at the right time, as soon as possible today! Reporters have lots of practice writing fast to meet their deadlines. Whether a story breaks early or late in the day, they know their job. It's to gather the facts and write the story. If a reporter tells his boss that he didn't complete the late afternoon story because he writes better in the morning, the coffee in the break room ran out, or his muse was on vacation, he won't last long on the job. As a professional writer, his job is to tell the story and do it fast.

Odds are, you're not a reporter, but if you happen to know one, you know their secret to writing fast. It's their job, and they have to get the work done. Assuming you're not a reporter, I encourage you to start thinking like one. Challenge yourself to practice writing at all times of the day, without waiting around for a visit from your muse. The difference between a hobbyist and a professional has to do with their commitment to getting a set amount of work done, such as the draft of a chapter within a set timeframe, or to write for a set amount of time every day, regardless of how they're feeling on any particular day. You don't have to be a full-time writer to work like a professional.

It's helpful to know what times of day work best for your writing. This isn't entirely about whether you're part of the 5 AM club or the night owl club; it has more to do with your best available energy on any given day. Consider how you can have an energy spike at any time of the day if something arouses your attention. Ideally, your book stimulates your attention. If you can keep your focus and attention on your book throughout the writing process, then your reader is more likely to stay interested as well.

In addition to paying attention to your energy and your ideal time of day to write, it's also important to consider the routines of those around you and in your space. Taking into consideration all your responsibilities, obligations, and normal patterns of eating, bathing, working, and sleeping, where does writing best fit in? Many writers write in the daytime or evening, while others find it best to wake up very early to write or stay up after everyone else in the household gets in bed. These household routines can change seasonally, and they can change over time, so it's important to always be open to making adjustments.

You are the only one who can define your best time to write. You know your energy patterns throughout the day. For example, I'm a writer and an entrepreneur. If I spend the day working on a lot of computer tasks, such as updating my website, doing SEO on blog posts, and answering emails, my creative battery will be drained. So, it's better if I write before doing this sort of work, or at least add margin and time to recharge after I remove my entrepreneur hat.

Regardless of when you choose to write, it's best to make it a habit, a part of your daily life, especially when working on a book. Engaging with your outline or manuscript daily will keep it fresh on your mind, and your subconscious will work on the book day and night, including when you're sleeping or working on other tasks. As you're presented with challenges of coming up with transitions or filling in areas that need more details or elaboration, your subconscious will continue to work to fill the gaps. If you work on your book, even a little, day after day, you will gain unstoppable momentum. I dare you to try this strategy. You won't regret it.

Minimizing Distractions

If I ask an audience of writers to give me examples of things that distract them from writing, I will get all sorts of answers, such as "my kids," "my spouse," or "my job," for example. They'll rattle off all sorts of things in their outer world, overlooking that most writing distractions come from within. If you can keep your mind focused despite what's happening around you, you're well on your way to writing distraction-free.

A big part of having an effective writing system is having a place to write where you can minimize distractions, disruptions, and interruptions. Yes, location matters. Even if you're in a studio apartment, some areas will be more conducive to helping you stay focused. I speak from experience with this. I once lived in a first-level apartment in Gainesville, Florida. It had large windows that opened to a big courtyard with regular foot traffic. My desk was in front of the window where I could see out. When I see people, I get inspired. Most of the people walking by were students or professionals walking alone. From here, I could also see the sky and have a good view of the current weather conditions.

If that window had opened into a pool courtyard where people were playing music and talking, and where kids were playing in the pool, I wouldn't be able to accomplish much at all. I've tried to train myself to work through such circumstances, but to no avail. It simply doesn't work for me. I could do some light journaling, but I couldn't effectively edit a chapter of a book, for example.

When I can hear conversations, it's very difficult for me to hold my train of thought. It's not that I want to eavesdrop. I wish I could turn it off, but it's nearly impossible. It's the same way with written words or letters. When I'm driving down the road, I automatically notice license plates, billboards, road signs, and anything with letters. I'm a text-oriented logophile. My eyes are drawn to letters and words. Visual stimulation in the form of people or scenery helps me write, whereas cacophonous noises, conversations, and loud music make it nearly impossible for me to write.

Your Sources of Inspiration

Inspiration can come from a multitude of sources. It can be sparked by nature, art, people, music, literature, and places, just to name a few. You may not know why something inspires you, but you certainly know when something does. It captures your curiosity. It makes you wonder. It gives you a new insight.

You can be inspired by putting things in your environment, whether it's pictures of loved ones, avatars of the characters you're working on, or a mock cover for your upcoming book. Inspiration, for some, might be fresh flowers. Perhaps you have a photo of a mentor or hero on your screensaver, someone who inspires you to keep going.

All these things can positively impact your ability to write, but nothing compares to the inspiration you can receive through people. We are designed to be with people. Our bodies are reminders that we're meant to connect with others on every level: physically, mentally, and spiritually. We have tongues that facilitate our conversations and ears to listen to the words of others. We have arms to embrace each other and hearts to love one another. This, in itself, is inspiring.

Some of your greatest inspiration for finishing your book will come from people. And the means by which you can provide the most inspiration will be through your impact on others. The best way to find inspiration to keep writing is to be an active member of a writing community and participate regularly. One of the great powers you have as a writer is the ability to put words on paper that can endure beyond your lifetime, offering you a unique opportunity that others who never write things down may not experience. That is inspiring!

Navigating Detours in Your Writing Journey

Can a recreational vehicle (RV) be part of your writing system? Yes, indeed. This would be like asking a travel blogger if traveling is part of their writing system.

My husband and I have an RV. Over the years, we have planned countless getaways. Sometimes, we head out for a few days, and other times, we head out for a month or longer. We embark on each journey with high hopes of exploring new trails and scenic views. I love going out in nature to write. It recharges my creative battery and soothes my writing soul. However, the RV-getaway part of my writing system sometimes has glitches.

On a recent RV trip to Flagstaff, Arizona, we set out to camp in one of our favorite Ponderosa pine forests just outside downtown Flagstaff. However, we discovered that the road to the campsite was closed due to high fire danger. Our gut reaction to such detours is exasperation. Our plan was to camp on Bureau of Land Management (BLM) land, where you can camp for up to fourteen consecutive days.

Because the road was closed in the first camp area, we explored new forest roads in absolute darkness. I mean, it was pitch black. Yes, Flagstaff is officially recognized internationally as a dark sky city, after all. We drove very slowly through the dark on rocky dirt roads filled with giant puddles, hoping to avoid getting stuck. Despite the fact that our RV does not have four-wheel drive, we were determined to find another campsite. Eventually, we found another campsite, but it was much later than we planned to arrive. I lost several hours of time I intended to use for writing.

When we woke up in the morning and saw our surroundings, we were thrilled with the scenic 360-degree view of a pine forest animated with birds and squirrels to entertain our cats.

Writing journeys are much like RV road trips. You begin each writing project with high hopes that you'll have a great experience. Whether working on a short article or a long book, you're eager to explore a new intellectual trail. Sometimes the path is smooth. Other times, it's rough. As writers, we have a great advantage in life. We can have fun writing about the good times and write down the lessons we learned in the not-so-good times. Unpredictable detours often pave the way to growth, expansion, and wisdom. When you experience a glitch in your writing system, treat it as an invitation to adapt, learn, and evolve.

The Sound of Writing

When I'm working from my home office, I rarely have unexpected noise issues to deal with. However, if I'm writing in a coffee shop, park, or campground, I come prepared with my headset to block out noise as needed. These simple routines and habits can help position you for successful writing.

When I'm writing, I prefer silence or nature sounds such as birds, a stream, or ocean waves. In my home office, I have an air purifier that provides white noise that drowns out any noise coming from my husband's office, which is down the hall. When the wind blows, I can hear from my office the wind chimes hanging from a tree outside my window. This is a pleasant sound for me. I also hear the occasional vehicle drive by.

Some people like to play music when they're writing. I have a hard time writing when I'm listening to music with vocals. I've experienced some level of productivity listening to my instrumental playlists, but even that can be distracting. Sometimes, I get tired of a song, or I'm not in the mood for it, so I stop writing to skip the track or remove it from the playlist. It may seem like a minor disruption, but it's a disruption, nonetheless. Most of the time, I don't play music when I write–but when I do, it's usually an instrumental playlist that I've already vetted.

I've heard some writers say they can't work when they hear people speaking their native tongue, but they can work when they're around people speaking other languages. I've lived in three countries and traveled to dozens of others. I have a fascination with languages and trying to decipher meaning from sounds, so even hearing foreign languages makes it difficult for me to write. If I can tell what language they're speaking, I'll try to listen for any words I might recognize. I have met a few writers who like to listen to vocal tunes when they write, but this is a show-stopper for me. If I listen to music, it has to be instrumental.

The most important thing to remember here is to recognize what does and doesn't work for you. Pay attention to the things that distract you and position yourself in situations where you can minimize them as much as possible. More than once, I've heard members mention getting distracted by roof work when trying to write. This is a great topic to discuss with your writing community—to increase your awareness and to share ideas among fellow writers.

Perhaps you never paid attention to what sounds you want to hear when you're writing, but when you're involved in a writing community, these kinds of things come up in conversation. Gaining awareness of what background sounds work best for you is yet one more aspect of defining your writing system.

One of the members of our writing community, Colleen Grace Clabby, specializes in sound healing. She recently explained how she incorporates singing bowls into her writing practice. She often begins a writing session with her singing bowls and meditation. This is her way of clearing her mind before she starts writing.

The Scent of Writing

I'm sensitive to smells, and they do affect my writing. Although I don't drink coffee anymore, I love the smell of roasting coffee. It's an uplifting scent that transports me into the writing zone. I love the salty smell of the ocean and the smell of the Ponderosa pine forests in Flagstaff, Arizona. But when I'm not out on an RV adventure, I can't count on nature to supply the sensual inspiration, so I use essential oils.

I have a large collection of essential oils, and I experiment with different scents throughout my home. As I write this, I have cypress essential oil emanating through a diffuser, filling my office with a refreshing, earthy scent. Aromatherapy helps me stay grounded and pay attention to the present moment. Like burning a candle, I know that there's an end to the candlestick. I know that the diffuser has a limited amount of water that will run out. And I know that I have a limited amount of energy today before I need to sleep. What scents do you associate with writing?

Your Dynamic Writing System

No two writers have the same system for writing. Your writing system is as unique as your fingerprint. You may use the same word processing tool as another writer, but you have very different writing habits. You might share a common genre with a fellow writer, but the way you go about gathering and recording your notes could be completely different.

Some writers keep their chapters in separate digital files, while others keep their whole work in progress in one large file. If you discuss your writing system with fellow members of a writing community or with an accountability partner, this reflection and continuous improvement process is also part of your writing system.

Although you can buy notebooks, pens, and software tools to assist with your writing, you can't buy a writing system. It's something you design on your own, either intentionally or unintentionally. There are a few things to keep in mind regarding your writing system. First, it needs to work for you, and it doesn't matter if it works for anyone else. Second, it's important for you to understand and enjoy (as much as possible) all the phases of your writing process. Otherwise, you'll avoid or miss steps essential to finishing your book.

Consider making an outline of your writing system or journaling about it. Or, if you're somewhat analytical or visual, you might find it helpful to draw a flow chart of your writing process. If you're more auditory, you might find it helpful to discuss your writing process with fellow writers. If you're more of a sensory and perceptive person, imagine the feelings you experience during each phase of the writing process. Regardless of how you decide to write about or reflect on your writing system, you will benefit from gaining a conscious awareness of your system to know when and if you need to make changes to improve it. Evaluate your writing system regularly.

Not all parts of your writing system need to be documented. If you allow yourself the freedom to flow, you can't predict where it might take you. One of our members of Prolific Writers Life, Colleen Grace Clabby, takes cues from her spiritual guides regarding what does and doesn't belong in her book.

Some writers channel their books and give credit to another source that provides them with the words. Dr. Helen Schucman claims that she wrote voluntarily in response to a voice that wasn't vocalized and she didn't physically hear, but it rapidly prompted her with the passages of her book *A Course in Miracles*. She says that it couldn't have been her voice because the subject matter was unfamiliar to her. She described it as knowing what to write instead of hearing what to write.

My Writing System

My personal writing process starts by drafting in various ways. I begin with a rough outline of the book's concept and structure, which makes it easier to fill in the blanks. I type directly into the document and also use dictation, copying and pasting my spoken words.

As I write, the outline inevitably changes — some chapters get deleted, sections and chapters get moved around, and the book continues to transform.

Throughout the writing process, I check in with my progress almost daily by attending events with fellow Prolific Writers Life members. Talking about my project with fellow writers, sharing challenges, and highlighting what's working well boosts my motivation and keeps me moving forward. Not only do I enjoy the company of fellow writers, but I also often have one of my cats with me in my office. Occasionally, Namaste jumps on my lap to write with me.

I journal regularly throughout the process. When different ideas come to mind, I jot them down in my journal. I may refer to my journal while writing, as it often contains valuable insights and ideas I can include in the manuscript.

After completing the first draft, I print out a full copy of the book and get it bound at an office supply store. Seeing the beginning, ending, and table of contents in physical form helps me visualize it as a book. This method also prevents me from over-editing certain sections digitally while missing others. By taking the printed book to different locations, such as the poolside patio in my backyard or the open desert space outside our RV, I can read it as if it were someone else's book. This change in context helps me edit more effectively and gives equal attention to all areas of the book.

I use a red gel pen for initial edits, reading the book from start to finish. Later, I input these edits into the computer using a different color pen, black or blue, to indicate that I've completed the edits. This process helps me track my progress. I repeat this method multiple times, printing and reading the book repeatedly over several months. I have participated in critique groups for some of my books, but for this book, I had beta readers. Although it's optional, I recommend having your manuscript reviewed by beta readers before sending it to your editor.

While writing this book, I realized that my eyes were stressed from staring at a computer monitor. I did some research on how to reduce eye strain. After reading *Optimal Eyesight* by Esther Joy van der Werf and *Give Up Your Glasses for Good* by Nathan T. Oxenfeld, I added "swinging" and other eye exercises to my daily writing routine. Not only did this reduce my eye strain, but it also reduced my overall stress.

Of course, there are many nuances to how I write my books, but having a high-level view of my writing process is helpful. Each writer's process evolves, and I reserve the right to improve mine with each book. For example, in the middle of working on this book, I switched word processing systems to match my editor's requirements, which involved a learning curve but was ultimately worth it.

If I put a chocolate-covered Brazil nut next to my computer to remind me to return quickly, does this count as part of my writing system? Yes, indeed. It's part of my system this week.

One night, after I had already released the book to my beta readers, I had a flood of stories and ideas come to me. I kept getting out of bed and walking to my office over a dozen times to add details to the book, including this one. I mentioned this to Dinara Jayakody, one of the members of the Prolific Writers Life community. She reminded me that it might be easier to keep my journal on my nightstand so I didn't have to keep getting out of bed. Sure enough, I had an abundance of ideas the next night, but this time I could jot down the notes in my journal without getting out of bed.

Although this blurb gives you a glimpse into my writing system, there's so much more involved, and it changes depending on the circumstances of any given day, whether I'm at home or traveling in my RV, for example. Managing the dynamic nature of the writing life is why we need to get together in a coworking community such as Prolific Writers Life. I look forward to seeing you there and hearing how your writing system is evolving.

Trust Your Instinct

Your intuition is that natural response to anything that is going on around you. You don't have to think hard about it. You know it's affecting you, and if you're in tune with your inner wisdom, you'll immediately know how you want to handle the situation. Pay attention to your internal guidance. Your intuition is your best guide. It's wise to get ideas from fellow writers, but ultimately, it's up to you to fine-tune your writing system until it feels right for you. When your writing system is working for you and keeping you on track with your writing goals, you'll be the first to know. The best evidence of the success of your writing system is your finished book.

In 2004, four years after I married a widower with five children, I started working with a writing coach, intending to write a self-help book. Intrigued by my courage to step into a family with five kids, she encouraged me to write about it. She assured me that it was a hot topic that could sell. I respected her and followed her advice. Over the course of several months, I ended up with enough content for a book, but I realized it wasn't the path I wanted to take. This experience taught me to trust my intuition when it comes to both the content of my writing and the writing process I follow.

As you become more aware of your writing system and what works for you, the next step is to focus on sustaining your writing flow from start to finish. This involves learning how to keep your momentum going throughout the entire process, which is the topic of the next chapter.

CHAPTER 6

Sustaining Your Flow from Start to Finish

The three most difficult parts of writing a book are getting started, maintaining momentum, and finishing strong. Compared to this, everything else may seem easy. But how is it that these three simple steps can be so complicated?

Writing a book can be as thrilling as it is daunting. Each step is crucial to see your book through to publication and beyond. Think about it like this: first, you develop your book idea and stick with it. Then, you keep that momentum going, working diligently through each chapter. Finally, you push through to the end, completing your manuscript and preparing it for the world to read.

I've met many writers along the way, each with their unique strengths and struggles. Some are brilliant at coming up with ideas and diving right into the writing process, but then falter when it comes to keeping the momentum. They get sidetracked by new ideas or lose steam halfway through. Others can maintain their momentum for a while, diligently working through their drafts, but stumble when it comes to finishing the manuscript and moving into the final phases of revising and publishing. Then there are those who never quite get started the right way, unsure how to outline their book or define their purpose and audience, resulting in wasted time and effort.

This book is a testament to the entire writing journey. It's for anyone who has started many projects or even worked on one for a long time but hasn't seen it through to completion. We explore what it takes to get started correctly, maintain that vital momentum, and finally bring your manuscript to completion. By the end, you'll be equipped with the knowledge and strategies to overcome obstacles at any stage of your writing process and transform your idea into a finished book ready to move on to editing and publishing.

Getting Started

The habits and tendencies you pick up throughout your life also impact your writing life. Some people dive in and try to write a book fast, while others take their time to research and learn as much as possible about the process of writing a book. Are you the type of person who dives into the deep end or one who walks in slowly at the shallow end of the project pool?

If it's your first book, you might not have any idea where to get started. Should you make an outline, start journaling, go to a writing workshop, or what? If you're a newbie, you may not know where to start, and you may not even know what questions to ask about getting started.

If you have already published other books, getting started on the next book has other reasons for being difficult. Now that you know how much work it is, you know how much time and effort you have to invest in the project to bring it to completion, and this might feel daunting. Are you committed to doing it all again? And will your next book live up to your prior one?

Some people have a hard time starting a book because they're writing about a distressing life experience, filled with pain and heartbreak. While you know your potential readers share similar experiences of loss or trauma, when you decide to write about it, you're committing to relive it, and hopefully, in the end, grow or heal as a result of processing it through the written word. In this case, you need a strong why to keep going. Your desire to help others needs to overpower your resistance to reminisce through these experiences repeatedly, as you find the words to tell your story.

Perhaps you're in your twenties and you feel you don't have enough experience to write a book. Not true! Or, you've been wanting to write a book for decades and just never got started. Our daughter, Amanda, reminds me that one of our favorite authors, David R. Hawkins, did not embark on becoming a prolific writer and published author until after the age of 60, after which he published over a dozen books. You are not too old or too young to get started. Now is a great time to start writing a book.

Regardless of your experience as a writer, you can look to fellow writers in a writing community for the support and encouragement you need to get started on your book.

Share Strategies and Get Guidance

It can feel defeating to hear the same advice repeatedly, such as "schedule a time to write every day," or "stick to your schedule," or "write a thousand words per day." It's easy to say, but not easy to do when you have a block. Some people call it writer's block, but if you're blocked with your writing, it's likely a symptom that you're also blocked elsewhere in your life.

You may have heard this time management advice for writers, but you can't seem to make it work for you. Perhaps you're in a state of overwhelm and can't figure out how to escape.

- Commit to writing for a set amount of time every day. *That might work for some people, but my daily routine tends to be different every day.*
- Set realistic writing goals. *Huh? This is my first book, so how would I know what's realistic?*
- Set deadlines. *I do, but I never keep them.*
- Schedule time to write. *I tried this, but other things always seem to come up.*
- Get professional help from a writing coach. *I don't know how to find the right one, and I don't know if I can afford it.*
- Minimize distractions and obligations. *I have many hobbies, interests, and obligations, and it's hard to find time for them.*
- Find an accountability partner. *Good idea, but I'm not sure if I'm ready for this.*

When you're part of a writing community and you hear fellow writers saying why they can't find the time to get their writing done, it's like looking in a mirror. You can relate. You've been there, and maybe you're still there. But it's very powerful hearing them talk through their challenges related to time.

For some reason, it always seems easier to encourage other people to overcome their challenges than to overcome your own. In the meantime, little by little, you realize that you have two options. You can keep doing things the way you've always done them, or you can get advice and try out new strategies. Choose the latter and try something new today.

Julie Powell, living in New York and frustrated with her job, decided to embark on an exciting cooking project: to prepare all 524 recipes in Julia Child's *Mastering the Art of French Cooking* within a year. She combined this challenge with a blog, where she documented her journey and shared her daily cooking experiences. What started as a personal project soon attracted attention, as readers became interested in her progress. This unexpected interest provided her with a powerful source of accountability, motivating her to keep going even when the task seemed daunting. Her blog eventually led to a book, which was later adapted into the movie *Julie & Julia*. This story highlights how combining your project with a platform for community support can create powerful momentum, helping you achieve your goals and turning your efforts into something greater than you initially imagined.

Where Does the Time Go?

Back in 2018, at the advice of one of my coaches, Minette Riorden, I kept a time log of everything I did for two weeks straight. This is not an easy task! I used an app that allowed me to enter custom categories of activities such as writing, editing, housekeeping, meal preparation, eating, sleeping, and so on. Each time I switched activities, I tapped the category to activate a time tracker for that category. The app even allowed for multitasking such as listening to an audiobook while preparing meals. In this case, I could tick off two categories at the same time.

This exercise turned out to be an eye-opener for me. One of my biggest revelations was that I put a lot of hours into grocery shopping, meal preparation, eating, and doing dishes. In fact, food turned out to be one of my top time-consuming activities. I had no idea how much time this was consuming each week. I'm vegan. I shop for organic produce and make homemade meals, but I wasn't aware of how much time this involved in food-related activities.

If someone had asked me to name my top time-consuming activities before I did this exercise, I would not have predicted this outcome. After going through this exercise, I started making larger portions so I could have leftovers for the upcoming days. This helped to free up more time to write and build the foundation for Prolific Writers Life.

If you're searching for ways to find more time to write, I encourage you to do a time log for two weeks and see where your time is going. It may give you some insights into how to free up more time to write.

Share your time log experience with fellow writers. Not only will this give you the motivation to get started, but it will also give you accountability to continue for the two weeks. You can also review your findings with fellow writers who can help you stick to any new habits or routines you want to implement. Unless you decide to hire a ghostwriter, it's up to you to seize time each day to write so you can finish your book.

Break Free from Over-Planning

As an organized person, I must admit that sometimes I over-plan. However, the benefit of being part of a writing community is having fellow writers observe my journey. They let me know when I'm stalling out in the planning process. There's no need to feel uneasy about this. It's a powerful form of self-reflection. Other writers often recognize in you what they've seen in themselves. Fellow writers can sometimes push you to the edges of your comfort zone, but this is the very thing that will help you grow and finish your book.

If you've been stuck in the outlining phase or on one chapter for the past six months, it's beneficial to get a nudge from fellow writers. It's important to recognize when it's time to transition from outlining and planning to writing and finally editing. When you share your progress with your peers, they can provide encouragement to propel you forward. This is one of the greatest advantages of working within a community.

Another pitfall some writers fall into is excessive scheduling or attempting to meticulously plan every aspect of their book launch or marketing strategy before the book is even written. While planning is essential, over-planning can result in unnecessary delays, defeating the purpose of planning altogether, especially if you miss out on opportunities. It's best to execute rather than analyze every detail. Your writing community can help you to keep moving forward rather than succumbing to getting stuck in a cycle of over-planning while sacrificing momentum.

Be Intentional: Set a Specific Goal

One of the most effective ways to boost your momentum is to approach your writing with a clear intention. Begin by setting specific, well-defined goals. For instance, you can state, "I want to write a book about ___ for my target audience to help them learn how to ___."

In addition, establish a target date for when you want to complete the book. "I want to complete this romance novel by ___ (insert date) to ensure it's available for a release date of January 14, one month before Valentine's Day, in ___ (insert year)." The more specific you can be, the better. Keep your goal at the top of your mind by putting it in a place where you can easily read it daily.

Coincidentally, I recently spoke with two authors (who didn't know each other) who had set a goal to write and publish their next books in time for upcoming speaking engagements, one for a writer's conference, and the other for a business keynote. They envisioned themselves at the live events, ready to present their talks and sign books at the end of the gathering. Having a vision like this can serve as a powerful motivator.

Having a clear picture of what you want to write is essential. If you're unsure about your intention, being part of a writing community can help solidify your goal. I know a writer who had three-inch-thick note-books filled with trail notes from his hikes at national parks across the United States. For decades, he had been on a personal quest to hike as many trails as possible. Along the way, he took stunning photographs and jotted down detailed trail notes about his experiences, mainly for himself. It was only later in life that he began to feel a strong desire to pass these memories down to his children and grandchildren, and perhaps even beyond. However, he wasn't sure how to transform this personal archive into something meaningful.

Once he joined a writing community, he gained the clarity he needed. Through discussions with other writers, he saw how his trail notes could come together in a blog, allowing him to showcase his amazing photos, while the book could focus more on his journal entries and the stories behind them. Initially, he wanted to publish his journals in book form, but with advice from established authors, he decided to first publish his articles and photos on a blog. This approach would allow him to refine the message he wanted to deliver in the book, without the cost-prohibitive nature of publishing a book filled with colorful photos. Once he realized that the blog could feature as many photos as he wanted, it freed him up to focus on storytelling in his book. He also discovered that the blog could be a powerful marketing tool for the book, helping him reach a wider audience.

Maintaining Momentum with Community Structure

In a writing community, a structured framework provides a means for productive communication among fellow writers. Workshops and work sessions offer opportunities to check in and discuss your progress. Work sessions provide dedicated time for focused work. These work sessions are especially effective because you can interact in real-time. You can ask questions and receive answers right away. This just-in-time approach allows you to get the answers you need when you need them, avoid getting stuck, and continue to make progress with confidence that you're moving in the right direction. The Words Count writing sessions led by Keiko O'Leary, Linton McClain, Maya Carlyle, Ryan Christopher, Liza Olmsted, Rod Sanford, Tanya Brockett, and even me were instrumental in helping me maintain momentum with my writing.

Work sessions take the collaborative spirit of a writing community to a whole new level. During these sessions, writers gather not just to listen and learn but also to write. Whether you complete one paragraph or free write 1,000 words, work sessions offer a chance for friendly accountability and a space to recognize your recent accomplishments.

This unique structure sets writing communities like Prolific Writers Life apart from informal gatherings where distractions can easily arise—whether it's the noise and interruptions at a café, the unexpected demands of a family member at home, or the time-consuming effort of commuting to in-person meetings. Or, consider the more formal gatherings such as conferences where writers rush from one session to the next and, ironically, have no time to write at all. Writing communities offer a powerful and purposeful coworking experience. The unique structure of a writing community cultivates learning, trust, camaraderie, and lasting friendships that often extend well beyond the book-writing process.

In a writing community, workshops and work sessions are indispensable for enhancing your productivity and refining your writing skills. Workshops provide valuable opportunities for you to expand your knowledge, improve your craft, and avoid pitfalls. Participating in a writing community is a sure-fire way to refine your writing skills and supercharge your productivity.

The Dynamic Nature of Writing

When writers say they're writing, they could be doing one of many things. The writing process is dynamic. It's not a linear process. It's circular and cyclical. Ultimately, we're practicing putting words together into sentences and sentences into paragraphs.

At any given time, a writer could be working on an outline, crafting a first draft of a manuscript, revising, or doing a combination of writing and revising simultaneously. Many experts advise against this, but writers will be writers. As writers, we have the freedom to work however we want.

Writers might claim they're writing when, in reality, they're building their platform. This includes posting on social media, blogging, and updating the copy on their websites. All these activities fall into the realm of "writing" because they involve creating content for books, articles, blog posts, or marketing materials. These are forms of writing, but they're outside the scope of writing a book. Workers say they're "working," and they could be working on almost anything. The same is true for writers. While they might say they're writing, it often means that they're simply doing the work of a writer, but not necessarily working on their current manuscript.

Writers are perceived as introverts who work in solitude. However, working in a community, especially when the community offers writing work sessions, can be essential for optimizing your writing process, habits, and routines. When you vocalize what you're working on, share your challenges, and discuss life's distractions and interruptions, fellow writers who truly understand the writing process can offer valuable insights and support.

Fellow writers can relate and have different experiences that they can share with you. Sometimes, a tip from a fellow writer can be so valuable to you and result in a big boost to your productivity. Returning to your writing community to write on a regular basis will help you expand your possibilities as a writer and increase your growth and productivity.

Deadline Drama: Facing Unexpected Plot Twists

The day I had planned to write this section about momentum started with a slip and a slam. I freed up a whole weekend to work on my book. Then, early afternoon one Saturday, I took some time out to mop my kitchen floor. I know, you might be thinking I shouldn't have been doing housecleaning on a day when I planned to write. On the contrary, I find it satisfying to load dishes in the dishwasher, hang wet clothes on the line to dry, or do some housecleaning to break up my writing sprints.

Anyway, I decided to mop the floor. I used a little too much soap on the mop, and the floor was super slick. As I was walking out of the laundry room over the slippery, wet tiles, the mop handle caught on the door. It was just enough to make me lose my balance, and I went straight to the floor, all my weight landing on my left wrist.

I rarely deal with headaches in my life, let alone a throbbing arm. This threw off my productivity for not only Saturday afternoon, but also nearly all of Sunday, on a weekend I had planned to make progress on my book. The good news is that, no matter what happens, it always turns into a story for a writer. Whether it seems good or bad, you'll have something to write about in the end.

Most professional writers stick to a schedule. They don't plan writing marathon weekends. I know better, but I had agreed to a tight publishing deadline. Since I'm not usually dealing with physical issues that hinder my productivity, it felt like fate had a message to deliver: Some people write through pain or other equally disruptive physical challenges regularly.

I trust that things happen for a reason. Thankfully, this turned out to be a short-term discomfort that only lasted for about two weeks. Within two days, I was able to start typing again. It was also a reminder to appreciate my good health and have compassion for others who work through pain. I was happy to have the support of my community, who empathized with my short-term setback. Instead of making my sore wrist an excuse for not writing, I focused on healing and returned to writing a few days later when it was comfortable. It's wise to have a target date for when you want to complete your book and to build in a margin for unforeseen circumstances such as this.

Finishing What You Start

It's hard to build a house when you don't have blueprints. Likewise, if you're not sure what it takes to write a book, not only is it difficult to get started, but it's also nearly impossible to accomplish without some guidance and direction. Without a blueprint and the know-how to start building, writers face all sorts of challenges. Some writers come into a writing community with a partial draft but aren't sure how to proceed. Other writers have several books they've started but procrastinate on completing them. Some have hand-written chapters in notebooks and don't have the technical skills to transfer them into digital files.

One of the great reasons to join a writing community is that it gives you access to people who can recommend reputable book coaches. A good coach can help you sort through your projects and decide which book to focus on right now. Creative minds prefer to explore and wander, so committing to one project means that you're going to give up time wandering so you can focus on completing one project. Many creative people are good at starting projects, but not necessarily at seeing them through to the end. Because they're com-pulsive starters, they can't focus on finishing any of them. Full disclosure—this is me. You're reading this book right now because I was supported by a commu-nity of good friends, my fellow writers, and experts in the Prolific Writers Life community who cheered me on and filled in gaps where I lacked finesse. I'm so grateful for the fellow members who shared this writing jour-ney with me.

Overcoming Procrastination

While you likely know when you're procrastinating, you may not be conscious of why. It's essential to be mindful of this phenomenon.

One valuable aspect of a writing community is that it provides a platform to discuss your procrastination tendencies with fellow writers. Many of them will relate. And they'll also ask good questions that help you determine the underlying cause. With encouragement from fellow writers, you can remedy your procrastination and move toward being a more productive writer. I've seen it happen countless times.

I hit a wall with one of the chapters while editing the third draft of this book. I thought it was because I was too busy taking care of business, but ultimately, I realized it was because I was stressing out about the book launch, which created a mental block for me. I had to stop thinking about the future phase of the book and focus on my current writing phase. Once I realized this, I finished the edit within a few days and went on to edit the fourth draft a few days later.

The antidote to procrastination is action. Openly engage with your writing community and consider the potential solutions offered by fellow members. Experienced writers and coaches in the community, such as book doulas or coaches, can help you take action and finish your book.

How Long Does It Take to Write a Book?

I have seen people come into the community who have been working on a book for years, and some bring book ideas they started over ten years ago. People hesitate to move forward on their manuscript for all sorts of reasons: they had a harsh editor tear their book to pieces and got discouraged; they wrote chapters, but didn't have the confidence to publish; they wrote the book, but didn't know how to go about publishing.

But once they get the support they need in the Prolific Writers Life community, they can finish writing their books and then publish them. In some cases, this happens over a very short period. I've seen people finish books in as few as four months, while others take over a year. They review and organize the manuscript they've been working on for years, pull it all together, review it, and do what it takes to get their book out.

In other cases, people have just been talking about writing a book, but simply getting into a writing community gives them the boost they need to start writing that first draft. It's transformative; they shift from the desire to write to having written, and this is a state that so many writers want to get to, from the desire to share a story to having shared the story in the form of a book.

Your fellow writers will lift you up, honor your achievement, and gladly spread the word when your book is released. Members of the Prolific Writers Life community have published incredible books, including Keiko O'Leary's *Your Writing Matters* (August 2022), Mary Pascual's *The Byways* (June 2023), Lyndley Fehr's *How to Clear Your Energy & the Energy of Others* (November 2023), Linton McClain's *Doing the Work* (November 2023), David Hern's *How Not to Make it in Hollywood* (May 2024), and Rod Sanford's *The Ex of My Ex* (September 2024) published under his pen name Carmen Ejuma, just to name a few.

Once your book is out, no one will care how long it took you to write it. Don't worry about how long it takes to finish your book. The most important thing is that you're working on it today and you're making progress toward your goal.

CHAPTER 7

Expect Surprises

I'd like to introduce you to a writer I know. She had high hopes for publishing her first book. She was elated when she signed a contract with a hybrid publisher. She didn't read the fine print on the contract, but she did expect them to help market her book. Although the publisher offered minimal support with the book launch, she was disappointed that they didn't offer any follow-up marketing support. After the book was published, she didn't hear from them for over a year.

When she finally heard from them, it was an impersonal email letting her know that they were going to start charging her a monthly fee for the unsold copies of her paperback stored in their warehouse. You might have heard a similar story or perhaps experienced something like this firsthand. Stories like this instill doubt and make you wonder if it's worth all the trouble.

Pay Attention to Your Expectations

When you face a plot twist in your writing journey, it's easy to get disheartened. Yet, these setbacks are seeds for unexpected growth. Expectations are tricky. It's like trying to do your own weather forecast. Sometimes you're right, and sometimes you're not. Budding writers don't know what to expect. In the process of writing, publishing, and promoting a book, we need to tread lightly with our expectations. It's essential to be optimistic about your writing journey, and it's equally important to ground your expectations to save yourself from frustration and disappointment. The best way to avoid surprises is to surround yourself with a community of writers, authors, and experts who can help you anticipate what's coming next.

What to Expect When You're Writing a Book

Ever heard of the popular book, *What to Expect When You're Expecting* by Heidi Murkoff? Just as no two pregnancies are the same, no two writing journeys are the same. Ironically, the process of going through pregnancy and birthing a baby is more predictable than the process of releasing a book. That's why there's a plethora of books and coaches on writing, publishing, and promoting your book. The purpose of this book is to help minimize your surprises and reduce your stress during your book's pregnancy, i.e., all that happens prior to its release. Do people really get pregnant with books? Yes, this is real. In fact, there are book doulas who will help ease you through the process of birthing your book. Being pregnant with a book, however, is not a physical experience. It's mostly mental.

You'd think that there would be one step-by-step plan to follow, but your book's journey will be different from everyone else's. Authors and experts have their systems and perspectives. Books such as the one you're reading now are valuable resources, but keep in mind that your journey will have its own twists and detours. You can't predict the surprises and setbacks that might come your way in your writing journey, so it's important to keep learning and remain open-minded and resilient.

Share your surprises and setbacks in a writing community. This is the best place to get answers to your questions on a just-in-time basis. Just-in-time help, available on an as-needed basis, is one of the greatest advantages of a writing community.

Dancing with Distractions, Disruptions, Interruptions, and Setbacks

Understanding what pulls you away from writing is crucial. Once you're aware of these obstacles, it becomes easier to address them in the moment and find your way back to writing. Distractions are temporary diversions of your attention and are often the easiest to manage since they're not urgent—you can develop strategies to reduce them. Disruptions, on the other hand, break your workflow and concentration, testing your patience. They are harder to handle because they're less predictable or controllable. Interruptions demand immediate attention and can't always be avoided, while setbacks present significant obstacles that delay progress and often involve physical or mental strain. Each type of obstacle requires a different approach to overcome.

Let's explore these challenges in more detail and look at strategies to handle them effectively.

Minimize External Distractions

Life is what's happening when you're writing. Distractions remind you of this. "Hey, I know you want to write, but I'm here to remind you that you still have a life." Distractions are like dance partners that join in uninvited. Whether it's a text message, a knock on the door, or a barking dog, they'll find you. Distractions can be particularly annoying when you're in the flow and need mental focus to compose coherent sentences and paragraphs.

Distractions can be both internal and external. External distractions come in the form of noises, notifications, people talking, and so on. Internal distractions come in the form of daydreaming, worrying, or thinking about what you will do later in the day. If you give in to distractions too often, such as checking your phone for a notification, you could easily get lost in social media, turning your attention to responding to an email, or heading out for a walk with your dog during a time you had intended to write.

How should you deal with distractions? Here's a tip I picked up from being an active member of the Prolific Writers Life community. This insight didn't come from a particular person, but from observing writers sharing stories about their distractions during Words Count writing session check-ins. Writers often express frustration about the distractions that arise during their writing time, while fellow writers find humor or positive aspects in the distractions or encourage them to let them go and move on.

Don't fight distractions; go with the flow. Treat them like little love notes from your muse. Welcome them, along with the lessons they've come to teach you. That cat walking across your keyboard may be a reminder that it's time to give your eyes a break from the computer. Did you just get a text message from a fellow officer in a nonprofit reminding you of your upcoming volunteer duties? Your stress level rises. Before replying, stop and take a deep breath. Perhaps the underlying message is hinting that it's time to step down from that volunteer role so you can free up more time to write.

Instead of tightening your eyebrows at distractions, train yourself to look at them with interest, as if they're private direct messages from your greater consciousness. They're sending you subtle invitations to tweak some aspect of your life today so that every following day can get better and better. If you're searching for the deeper meaning of a distraction, bring it up in your writing community, and you will, most likely, get all sorts of potential synchronicities, especially if they know you well. Your gut instinct is most important in these situations. When you share your distractions with fellow writers, they may offer insights that you never considered.

Seek Support to Manage Internal Disruptions

Sometimes disruptions are subtle. Have you ever had emotions bubble up unexpectedly and hijack your attention? I've known many writers who were working on memoirs or sharing true stories of personal trauma or tragedy. I've seen them wrestle with scenes in their books that make them cry or give them emotional bruises for days or even weeks. Obviously, this can affect their writing flow. Likewise, I've seen writers editing traumatic scenes from their past, saying that it feels like it happened in a different lifetime. It doesn't trouble them anymore. Others say that they still feel the pain, but they now understand why this happened to them. They continue on because they feel called to help others going through similar circumstances. In many cases, they can see, in retrospect, that it opened up new opportunities for them or changed their lives in a powerful and ultimately positive way.

Even when you're not writing an emotionally charged story, unexpected feelings can surface. Whether you're grieving the recent loss of a loved one or feeling elated about an upcoming wedding, strong emotions can consume your mental bandwidth. Many creatives find that in moments of intense emotion, both sorrow and joy, their artistic expression becomes a vital outlet. For example, Eric Clapton co-wrote the song *Tears in Heaven* in 1991 after the tragic death of his four-year-old son. In the midst of overwhelming grief, song-writing became a way for him to process what he was feeling. Learning to recognize and channel your own emotional energy, whatever form it takes, into your creative work can lead to some of your most powerful writing.

Regardless of where you are on the emotional rollercoaster of life, it can impact your writing. Whether you're up or down or somewhere between, fellow writers can relate. Acquiring strategies to manage your emotions could be the very thing that can help you reach your writing goal, without which you might attempt to run away, only to find that you regret it later. If you're not prepared to share your inner turmoil, write in your journal to vent and share it later when and if you're ever ready. Journaling is almost as powerful as having the full attention of a good friend, so take advantage of this powerful tool for writers. Find a writing community where you can surround yourself with fellow writers who encourage and support you through both good and bad times.

Expect the unexpected. Disruptions don't ask for permission to show up. Your internet could go down when you're trying to do fact-checking online. By participating in a writing community, you can be better prepared to adapt and find strategies so that disruptions don't derail you from making progress on your writing.

Put a Positive Spin on Disruptions

A disruption is more severe than a distraction. It diverts your attention and breaks your workflow. Perhaps you're writing in a coffee shop and a neighbor seizes the opportunity to fill you in on the details of a recent incident that happened in your neighborhood. Or you're working from home at night and experience a power outage. In either situation, it can be difficult to resume your focus. Try to put a positive spin on disruptions. What can you extract from them? That power outage is here to trigger a great idea for a scene in your book. And you're reminded yet again that writing in the coffee shop closest to home might not be the ideal place to work. And, oh yeah, you've been wanting to cut back on coffee anyway because it's affecting your sleep. The library might be a better option.

The Benefit of Interruptions

One day, I was in a Words Count writing session with fellow Prolific Writers Life members. When it came time for me to check in with my progress, I slumped my shoulders forward, confessing that I got interrupted and didn't accomplish the writing task I set out to do. A neighbor knocked on our door to let us know that she saw a puddle in our front yard, which likely meant we had a leak in our irrigation system. I felt defeated and frustrated that my writing got interrupted, and I now had a house maintenance problem that needed to be resolved.

Keiko spoke up and said, "I know you try to protect your writing time from interruptions, but that's for non-urgent things. This interruption is helping you because it's urgent. You needed to find out about the leak right away so that you could take care of it before it gets worse."

I'll never forget this moment because it gave me a new outlook on interruptions. I now welcome them as invitations to snuff out sparks before they become flames. The guidance we receive from fellow writers often applies not only to our writing but to life in general.

Sometimes, interruptions aren't quite so dramatic, but they still impact our writing life. One time, my smoke detector battery started beeping when I was in the flow of writing, but I know it's a safety device that's tied into our security system, so I grabbed a stepstool and changed the battery.

When my husband texts me to see if I want him to pick up anything at the grocery store on his way home from a workout, I'm happy to respond because this saves me a trip to the grocery store and frees up more time for me to write.

Cultivate the habit of managing interruptions with a positive outlook. They're an inevitable part of every writer's life, so it's helpful to recognize them and have strategies to get back on track. When you're part of a writing community, you'll discover a plethora of strategies to deal with interruptions. One thing I love about writers is that they're creative people, and they can offer up countless ways to perceive the situation. Sharing your experiences and learning from fellow writers can help you maintain focus and productivity. Sometimes you get words of wisdom that create breakthroughs in your writing life.

And remember Curtis Chin? Out of necessity, he trained himself to go from one type of work to another — from working on an essay to seating customers, and then going back to working on his essay. Taking care of customers was of utmost importance to his family's business. Much of your success as a writer depends on your ability to adapt to the interruptions that come up in your unique life circumstances.

Take Time Out to Resolve Setbacks

A setback is a significant obstacle that impedes your progress and impacts your writing schedule or goals. Setbacks can be internal or external. For instance, if your computer crashes and you don't have a backup copy of your manuscript, this could be a major setback, causing a big delay as you rewrite your content. Internal setbacks can be physical, mental, and even spiritual. If a close family member passes away while you're working on your book, this could significantly delay your project. When facing a setback, give yourself the time and space to recover without putting unnecessary pressure on yourself. Adjust your goals and expectations and stay connected with your writing community. Take time to assess your situation and adjust your writing schedule. One word of caution: don't abandon your book. Stay connected with your writing community and let them know what you're going through. They can offer support during tough times.

Treat Surprises Like Valuable Opportunities

Every surprise you face, whether good or bad, is like a tiny gift from the universe, reminding you that you have a choice as to how you want to perceive it. Perhaps you sent out over fifty queries to find an agent but haven't received any response. Even if you expected to pursue traditional publishing for a long time, it's best to keep your options open. You can let challenges defeat you, or you can overcome them. Successful authors persevere through the problems and unforeseen circumstances that arise with each book they write.

If you want to finish your book, the best thing you can do is to surround yourself with a community of fellow writers and industry experts. They have ventured through the honored ritual of one or more book releases, and they can point you in the right direction. Chances are, you will be faced with decisions you didn't anticipate, but when you're in good company and have friends to depend on, you can get through the decision process with confidence and continue to make progress on your book.

The ROI of Writing Beyond Financial Gains

Statistically, most authors do not profit from books. But this doesn't stop writers from continuing with the next book and the next. Most writers do not embark upon a book project expecting to make money on the book alone.

Many authorpreneurs use their book as a way to introduce people to their ideas or their business. A published author is more likely to get a keynote speaking engagement than an equal counterpart who has not published. Likewise, a bestselling author is more likely to get booked for a TV, radio, or podcast interview than a fellow author who does not have a bestseller.

If you're looking for exposure in your field or to expand your reach, having a book is a great way for people to become familiar with what you stand for. It also provides credibility and helps you to stand out among your peers. Once your book is published, you will be surprised at the unexpected opportunities that come your way. I often hear authors share stories about how someone read their book and reached out to them with a raving review or an invitation they never anticipated.

When it comes to a book, in many cases, your return on your investment might not come in the form of money, but more so in the form of adding value to people's lives through self-help information or entertainment. And who knows...you might not be expecting to make much money on your book, but you might be pleasantly surprised at what comes your way as a result of finishing your book.

CHAPTER 8

How to Choose the Right Writing Community

Gardeners gather to swap seeds and share gardening secrets. Film producers attend film festivals to showcase their latest creations and connect with potential collaborators and distributors. Writers play with words. This alone provides countless reasons for writers to gather in various communities. For many years, writers have gathered with fellow writers to discuss their works in progress. The infinite combinations of words create endless meanings and possibilities, making every gathering a unique and enriching experience.

Being part of a writing community is all about building relationships, supporting one another, and being in a place where you can continuously learn from each other. It's not just a place to chat with like-minded individuals. It's a place to write, grow, and build lifelong friendships. It's an ongoing powwow where writers share tips, encourage each other, socialize, and recognize milestones. It's not a superficial interaction. An established writing community provides a place for deep connection and understanding. It's a place to share triumphs with fellow writers who care about your success.

I have truly come to understand the power of a writing community through various experiences. When I heard a veteran stand on stage in front of fellow writers to recite poetry about his horrific experiences at war and how PTSD destroyed his family, I understood the power of a writing community. When I witnessed a woman with one leg insist on getting on stage like all the other authors so she could give a talk to her fellow writers, I understood the power of a writing community. When I looked into the teary eyes of a mother whose son committed suicide and she struggled to preserve his life story in the form of a book, I understood the power of a writing community. When I saw a woman show up to give her writing workshop the day after her mother died, so she could keep her commitment to her fellow writers, I understood the power of a writing community. All of these authors had the strength to overcome tremendous obstacles because they were backed by a supportive writing community.

Why Writers Need Community

My family and non-writer friends don't understand my passion for writing. They provide occasional encouragement, but it doesn't compare to the deeper understanding I share with fellow writers. They know the creative process and all the challenges of bringing an idea to life by incorporating it into the written word. They understand how much effort it can take to persevere through the criticism and rejection you sometimes experience as a writer.

Throughout my writing life, I have found that I make much more progress when I have support from fellow writers. Writing a book helps you discover who you are, and writing a book in the company of fellow writers deepens your connection with your writing family.

How Writers Connect

Writing in solitude isn't the dream it's cracked up to be. In fact, writers who try to do everything on their own often make costly mistakes. It's important to know how much value you can gain by connecting with fellow writers. A writing community has the potential to transform your writing life into a fun adventure with like-minded comrades.

Although you might be aware of the various ways that writers connect, you probably never gave much thought to deciding which levels of connection work best for you throughout the different phases of your writing life. The following chart shows some examples of traditional ways that writers connect.

Quadrant #1: Fleeting Encounters

I classify the first type of writing gatherings as fleeting encounters because they provide the stage for short-term connections and shallow conversations. It's like speed-dating for writers. Because of their short duration, it limits the depth of the connections you can form. This is the case for conferences, book festivals, and open mics. They typically last for a few hours or a few days. Due to the limited time available, there is little opportunity to delve deeply into the exchange of information or build substantial relationships.

Authors and experts participating in these events often aim to promote their books or services. Consequently, interactions tend to evolve around sellers offering their services to potential buyers. It's possible to form lasting friendships at these events. However, the events do not provide a sustained platform for on-going connections unless you're an organizer or leader.

	Shallow	Deep
Short Term	Quadrant #1 **Fleeting Encounters** Book Festivals Writing Conferences Open Mics	Temporary Bonds Writing Retreats Alpha and Beta Readers Accountability Partners
Long Term	Enduring Connections Local Writing Groups Writing Associations Critique Groups	Deep-Rooted Kinship Hubs and other writing communities like Prolific Writers Life

Book Festivals

Venturing into book festivals offers a fun rendezvous with authors, readers, and book enthusiasts. These literary events, like the Tucson Festival of Books or the Amelia Island Book Festival, unite creative minds through a shared love of stories and ideas. Book festivals offer the opportunity to engage in panel discussions, ask authors about their creative processes, and purchase autographed books from big-name authors.

While book festivals can boost energy and insights, they're often fleeting, spanning just a day or two, making it a challenge to establish enduring connections. Participation is usually free for the general public and readers, but authors who want a booth need to carefully weigh the potential return on investment they might get from such events. Delve into book festivals for their camaraderie and inspiration, but recognize that sustaining bonds with the people you meet requires a lot of post-festival dedication. Book festivals can be a blast, but keep in mind that while you may meet some terrific people, it takes effort on your part to follow up and nurture the connections.

Writing Conferences

Writers' conferences are a whirlwind. You dive into workshops, learn from big-name panelists, mingle at the keynote dinner, and pitch your masterpiece. For a few days, you give up sleep and run on adrenaline. It's a rush of inspiration and connection, right? But here's the thing: while conferences can offer a jolt of inspiration, they also come with a cost and a clock ticking too fast. You gather business cards, postcards, bookmarks, and publishers' catalogs like souvenirs. Yet amid the buzz and endless introductions, lasting connections can be elusive. That avalanche of insights quickly fades as you re-enter the everyday writing grind. Conferences have their charm, but they're like fleeting fireworks — dazzling, but here today, gone tomorrow. Do I recommend going to writing conferences? Absolutely. However, if you're seeking unwavering camaraderie and support, you're better off investing your time in a writing community that stays with you through every chapter of your writing life.

Open Mics

Participating in open mics, whether virtual or live at a local coffee shop or bookstore, is a valuable practice for writers. One of the most important aspects of being a writer is to share your work with an audience. While critique groups and work sessions provide platforms for sharing, open mics offer a different experience. Attendees at open mics are open to hearing a variety of voices and perspectives. These events often feature a variety of performances from poets, musicians, storytellers, and writers.

Some open mics have specific themes, while others are more open-ended community gatherings. Regardless of the format, they provide a fantastic opportunity to engage with your community and potential readers.

167

It's a terrific venue to refine your public speaking skills. Participating in open mics offers numerous benefits. You get the chance to assess audience engagement. It gives you a reason to revisit and refine your work, thereby enhancing its quality.

You can adapt your writing into speeches within organizations like Toastmasters, which primarily focuses on public speaking. Toastmasters provides a platform for practicing your work through structured speech projects and impromptu speaking sessions. There are several types of Toastmasters clubs, including company clubs, college clubs, military clubs, and specialized clubs such as those for entrepreneurs or writers.

When you have the chance to get on stage, whether at open mics or similar venues, take advantage of the opportunity. It will help you become more productive and better prepared for future speaking engagements, such as podcasts or media appearances. Embrace open mics and public speaking opportunities as a valuable practice for becoming a more successful author.

Quadrant #2: Temporary Bonds

A second category of writing gatherings includes those that provide opportunities for short-term deep connections, such as writers' retreats, beta reader reviews, and accountability partnerships. In these situations, you can forge deep connections in a short amount of time. The duration could be a couple of days or possibly even a week or longer.

A beta reader is someone who reads a work-in-progress manuscript with the aim of providing feedback to the author regarding its strengths, weaknesses, and overall quality. If you ask someone to be a beta reader for your book, there's a chance you can forge a deep connection, especially if they're an ideal reader for your book, but there's no guarantee that the relationship will last very long. Likewise, if you make a deep connection at a writing retreat, there's a good chance you'll part ways and never talk again. If you're an accountability partner, you may have a deep understanding of the person's goals and objectives for a particular project, but the relationship can fall by the wayside after the project is complete. Despite the fact that most of these connections are likely to be short-lived, you never know when you might encounter someone who has a significant impact on your writing life.

	Shallow	**Deep**
Short Term	Fleeting Encounters Book Festivals Writing Conferences Open Mics	Quadrant #2 **Temporary Bonds** Writing Retreats Alpha and Beta Readers Accountability Partners
Long Term	Enduring Connections Local Writing Groups Writing Associations Critique Groups	Deep-Rooted Kinship Hubs and other writing communities like Prolific Writers Life

Writing Retreats

A writing retreat is a dream vacation for many writers. It's a chance to escape from everyday life and go off to write either alone or in the company of fellow writers. Participants have a common goal—to immerse themselves in their imagination and let the words flow. To enhance the ambiance, retreats are often held in picturesque settings, such as cabins in the woods, oceanfront hotels, or mountain retreats. Some people splurge and go on writing retreats abroad, adding another dimension to their experience.

In the summer of 2018, I attended a Morning Pages retreat with Julia Cameron and more than 100 participants at 1440 Multiversity in Scotts Valley, California. Julia is the author of forty books, but she's best known for her popular book, *The Artist's Way*. In this book, she encourages creatives to write three handwritten pages every morning to unblock creativity. She calls these Morning Pages.

We spent several days together, attending Julia's lectures and then having time on our own to write, reflect, and enjoy delicious organic farm-to-table meals with the other participants. This type of retreat is an excellent way to unplug from our normal lives and explore what writing means to us.

In this case, it was specifically focused on Morning Pages, with Julia sharing what the practice had done for her life and for so many others. We learned about the power of waking up and journaling three pages by hand each morning. The main purpose of the retreat was to fully understand her technique and how it's changed her life and the lives of countless creatives.

What stands out to me about this experience is the incredible bonds that formed so quickly. During the lectures, Julia would sometimes stop and ask us to form small groups to share our experiences with Morning

Pages journaling or discuss her teachings. I don't remember exactly what we were asked to talk about, but the point was that we were all sharing personal thoughts and insights.

It reminds me of a connection I once made on a twelve-hour international flight. I had a deep personal conversation with the woman next to me, and a few hours later, she fell asleep with her head on my shoulder. There's an energy and closeness that comes from being in tight quarters with other people, all of us experiencing something unique together. Julia's retreat was an incredible opportunity to dive deep, make meaningful connections, and truly understand the power of Morning Pages.

Although we formed meaningful connections during the retreat, they seemed to vanish the moment we returned to our everyday lives. That's the bittersweet nature of these experiences: they're intense and transformative, but often fleeting.

Writing retreats are alluring, but they often come with price tags that don't work for everyone. Making them a regular part of your writing life can be challenging due to cost, time constraints, and life commitments. But don't let this deter you. Attend retreats whenever possible to soak in valuable insights and techniques shared by seasoned writers. Then, bring that inspiration back into your daily writing routine–carry the retreat with you, in spirit and in practice.

Retreats offer the time and space to write and forge connections with fellow writers, get engrossed in deep conversations, and share from the heart. However, sustaining these relationships beyond the retreat can be slippery. While retreats help facilitate bonds, maintaining them requires intentional effort. Relish in the camaraderie while you can, but recognize that lasting connections demand time and ongoing interaction. If you're part of a virtual writing community like Prolific Writers Life, you'll have a space you can recommend to stay connected and continue the creative conversation long after the retreat ends.

Alpha and Beta Readers

Alpha readers are those who get an early look at your manuscript, sometimes even at its first draft stage. They might help with story structure and the overall development of the narrative. These readers are often close friends or critique group partners who are actively participating in your story as it unfolds. Therefore, it's crucial to carefully select who you allow into this role, as their feedback could significantly shape your book.

Beta readers, on the other hand, come into play once your manuscript has moved beyond the initial draft. By this stage, you've refined the story and completed some self-editing, likely reaching a second or third draft. Beta readers will see the full manuscript from start to finish and provide insights on readability, pacing, character development, and overall enjoyment. Their feedback is vital for polishing the final product, so selecting the right beta readers is equally important.

It makes sense to choose people who generally like to read in your genre, but you might also select some readers based on their area of expertise. Susanne Perry, author of the *City Streets Trilogy*, takes her beta readers very seriously. She has written several books featuring courtroom scenes and governmental institutions, drawing on her background as a social worker. She seeks out attorneys and individuals who work in these agencies to ensure accuracy in her storytelling. Depending on the story's focus, which often involves homeless characters navigating various systems, she enlists beta readers with relevant experience to ensure authenticity. Depending on your book's subject matter and audience, having beta readers who can provide input on authenticity, flow, and accuracy can be extremely valuable.

It's helpful to let beta readers know what you want them to look for. In general, beta readers look for issues they see in the book. They give you feedback on how engaging the book was for them. Plus, they can give you feedback on their overall reading experience.

Writers often choose beta readers from their own network, so this gives both the beta reader and writer a chance not only to catch up with their friendship but also for the beta reader to get intimately connected with the book. This can help to invigorate your friendship on a short-term basis.

It's equally important to seek beta readers who don't know you very well. People you're close to might hesitate to offer constructive criticism, whereas unfamiliar beta readers can provide a fresh perspective akin to that of a typical reader. Their feedback is more likely to mirror the reactions of strangers to your book, unlike that of friends or family, who may be biased. Whenever possible, aim to include beta readers who aren't familiar with you or your background.

Being an alpha or beta reader can be somewhat time-consuming, depending on how in-depth people go into reading your manuscript and providing feedback. Regardless, it's crucial to show appreciation to your readers for the time they invest in reviewing your work. Your beta readers, who are also writers, gain insights into their own craft by recognizing gaps and areas for improvement in your writing. For those who are readers but not necessarily writers, their motivation might come from enjoying the story or learning something new from your manuscript. Whether their involvement is driven by a desire to help or genuine interest, acknowledging their contribution is vital. A simple mention in your acknowledgments can go a long way, but think of creative ways to express your gratitude—every gesture of thanks enriches the collaborative process and strengthens relationships with those who support your writing journey.

Accountability Partners

When I lived in China, I met a fellow expat who was working on a book. The introduction came courtesy of our husbands, Matt and Bob, who were both consulting together at the same Huawei office in Shenzhen. Melissa Schneider was a blossoming counselor and was captivated by Chinese perspectives on marriage. To make use of her time in China, she decided to write a book on the subject. Around the same time, in 2012, I came across an article about how Hong Kong had surpassed Okinawa in having the highest percentage of centenarians in the world. This caught my attention, and I started writing articles and blog posts on the subject.

Melissa and I met at a coffee shop nearly every week for months. I provided feedback on chapters of her book, and she offered feedback on articles I wrote for my blog and the Shenzhen expat magazine. I enjoyed reading her growing collection of marriage stories. She often had funny quips about language challenges she had when doing interviews through translators. Plus, she always had surprising stories from the people who agreed to share intimate marriage experiences. Likewise, she enjoyed my adventures of traveling to Hong Kong and Okinawa to learn more about centenarians. She also appreciated the growing collection of health tips I accumulated from my research.

When Matt's consulting contract in China came to an end, they moved back to New Jersey, and she published her book, *"The Ugly Wife is a Treasure at Home: True Stories of Love and Marriage in Communist China."* One of the greatest lessons I inadvertently learned from Melissa is that she was wise to focus on one book and capitalize on her current life situation. Although I thoroughly enjoyed learning about centenarians, I didn't feel qualified to write a book, so I stuck with articles.

When Bob and I moved back to the U.S., all I had to show for my work were some dated articles in an expat magazine. Melissa had a book that applied to her career as a relationship coach. And this remains beneficial to her indefinitely.

Depending on your relationships, accountability partners can fall into any of the "How Writers Connect" categories, but they rarely fall into the deep and long-term category. Melissa and I had a deep connection through our friendship and writing projects for months, but we haven't worked on another writing project since we left China.

Quadrant #3: Enduring Connections

Writing groups and associations provide a means for long-term, shallow connections with fellow writers. These groups typically revolve around a shared theme, such as a specific genre, particular interest, or geographical location. They provide a structured environment for individuals to connect and mutually benefit from each other's experiences. People you meet can play significant roles in your writing journey.

	Shallow	Deep
Short Term	**Fleeting Encounters** Book Festivals Writing Conferences Open Mics	Temporary Bonds Writing Retreats Alpha and Beta Readers Accountability Partners
Long Term	Quadrant #3 **Enduring Connections** Local Writing Groups Writing Associations Critique Groups	Deep-Rooted Kinship Hubs and other writing communities like Prolific Writers Life

Local Writing Groups

Local writing groups have a unique dynamic. The knowledge within the group is shaped by the members directly involved, and it may also be influenced by their extended networks. While they might refer you to others, the scope of their guidance is mainly confined to their personal experience. This limitation carries the risk that if a particularly opinionated member offers guidance, it might not align with your specific needs. They have no intention of causing harm, but remember that their advice may be based on a few anecdotal stories they heard from fellow writers. Be cautious about taking advice from one person with limited experience.

Seek guidance from a variety of authors and experts who have a solid background in the writing industry.

As with any cross-section of a population, you'll meet mostly nice people, but occasionally, you'll meet someone naughty. When I lived in Florida, I was part of a local writing group that met at a residential location. One evening, when I left the meeting, I was one of the last people out the door. One of the men, a bestselling author who had published several crime thrillers, offered to accompany me to my car. It was getting dark, so I felt it was the gesture of a gentleman who had my well-being in mind.

I unlocked my car. He reached out and insisted on opening my car door. As I attempted to get in my car, he pressed his hips up against me and caressed my cheeks. He looked into my eyes intently and said something like, "I see how you bat your eyes at me. It's obvious you're attracted to me. I know you want me."

Although I frequently complimented him as a talented writer, I was happily married and had no interest in a fling. After a brief struggle to free myself, I convinced him that I was not interested in his proposition. The male characters in his books were philanderers, and, to my surprise, I discovered that he was just like this in real life too.

A few weeks later, when I was alone with one of the other ladies in the group, I watched her eyes open wide and her eyebrows rise as I told her my story.

She leaned forward and whispered, "Let me tell you what he did to me," she said, proceeding to share her story of how he made an unwelcome advance on her. "And we're not the only ones." She went on to tell me how he had made his rounds, hitting on other women in the group as well. And in some cases, he was even more savage. As time went on, we discovered that he was attending various writing groups and hitting on women all over town.

As word spread to the various group leaders and to the men in the groups, this womanizing rascal was eventually ostracized from the local writing community. I have no idea if his wife ever found out about his escapades. *How could she not know?* I wondered. But I was struck by how the local group leaders stepped up to protect the greater writer community. People from different groups, who normally didn't talk, suddenly had a reason to come together to protect the local flock of writers.

At the time, I remember appreciating how these subdivided groups recognized their common bond of looking out for fellow writers. I wanted to forge more connections among the fragmented groups, but I wasn't quite sure how to go about it. Plus, my husband was lining up an international contract position in China, and I wasn't sure how much longer we would be in the area.

Local writing groups offer a great way to connect with fellow writers, but they come with their own set of challenges and dynamics. Once, I was part of a writing group led by an author who also happened to be a real estate agent. Although he was a talented author, he always took up meeting time talking about his latest listings and asking for referrals.

While you can gain valuable insights and support, be mindful of the varied experiences and intentions of the members. Overall, local groups can be a great way to connect with fellow writers, but always seek a broad range of perspectives to enrich your writing journey.

Writing Associations

In many cases, writing associations are niche-oriented. They provide specialized information in a specific area, not necessarily considering how it aligns with the broader scope of your project or how it fits into the bigger picture of your writing journey. There are many types of writing associations, both for-profit and not-for-profit.

- Genre-specific, such as nonfiction, romance, or memoir
- Target-audience-specific, such as children's and young adult writing associations
- Goal-specific, such as self-publishing or writing a book to promote your business
- Education-oriented, such as professional writing associations
- Writer-specific associations, such as those created specifically for women, teens, or other audiences

You can enjoy lasting friendships in any of these associations. But recognize that although their information might go deep in a niche area, their information might not be as broad as you'd like. With narrow guidance, you can end up in a quandary, unsure of how to integrate it with the rest of your writing project and writing life. Or you might end up surrounded by people who have a constricted perspective of the world, which could limit your opportunities and creativity. Writing associations are a great place to do a deep dive, but remember to step back and gain a broader perspective by gathering with writers and authors through other venues.

Critique Groups

If you've ever been part of a critique group, you've probably felt like you were on a roller coaster. You show up at the regularly scheduled time and take a deep breath before passing around your latest chapter to be put to the test by your fellow judges. Over time, personalities emerge. You know who shows up early and who holds up the group because they often arrive late. You know who is going to be tough and who is going to be tender.

When done correctly by caring and perceptive individuals, it's possible to come out of a critique session feeling encouraged. But the danger with critique groups is that they can scare away those who haven't yet built up enough confidence with their writing. By design, critique groups are structured to enable people to help one another improve their work. However, they can be overrun by the revered few who have already published or, in some other way, set themselves as the authorities in the group. For these reasons and others, some critique groups can be shallow in the relationship-building arena, and there's always a risk of hurting feelings.

One of the biggest issues with critique groups, from my personal experience being involved in several, is that they can be time-consuming. I've been part of various groups where structured sessions initially worked well, but as more members joined, meetings inevitably stretched longer. What might start off as a manageable ninety-minute session can quickly extend to two to four hours or more, especially when discussing multiple submissions. There have been times when I found myself in critique sessions for up to four hours, where the whole group reads through and then does a round-robin of comments on numerous chapters. While this can be rewarding if you have the flexibility and enjoy the process, it might simply not be possible if you don't have that much time to spare.

Critique groups can be a touchy subject among writers. Some people are more in favor of them, and others are less so. The most important thing with a critique group is how it's led and how well-prepared participants are to provide critique and give positive feedback.

A few things to consider here are that the people in the critique group may not be ideal readers in your target market. This is a very real possibility if you're meeting with local writers who just happen to live nearby.

If you're in a writing association group, you're attending something within your genre. Members are potential readers of your book because they read and write in your genre. However, the downside to confining yourself to a genre-based group is that books all start looking and feeling alike. You have less chance of getting unique ideas that may come from someone who writes outside your genre.

When I first started going to critique groups, I felt out of place because I was often the only nonfiction writer in the group. At first, this bothered me, but the more I worked with fiction writers, the more I realized how much I could learn from them. I was in a group where there was a poet who suggested that a particular romantic scene would be a great opportunity to insert a love poem. On another occasion, a songwriter suggested that it might be interesting to mention what song was playing in a scene that takes place in a restaurant. And, on another occasion, I remember a children's book author picking up on a dialogue between a child and an adult. The children's book author recommended some revisions based on how a child that age would actually talk. The benefit of mixing in cross-genre critique groups is that you can get a range of perspectives. The cross-pollination is the very thing that spices up your writing style.

Quadrant #4: Deep-Rooted Kinship

After years of participating in all the previously listed writing gatherings, I couldn't help but think that there must be a way to forge connections between all these fragmented opportunities for writers, while also having a place to build deep, long-term connections with fellow writers. Over the course of several decades, I have exceeded well over 10,000 hours of studying and experiencing the writing industry as a passionate reader, an English professor, and a writer. However, it still felt like something was missing, and this inspired me to come up with a solution, which ultimately led to the creation of Prolific Writers Life.

	Shallow	**Deep**
Short Term	Fleeting Encounters Book Festivals Writing Conferences Open Mics	Temporary Bonds Writing Retreats Alpha and Beta Readers Accountability Partners
Long Term	Enduring Connections Local Writing Groups Writing Associations Critique Groups	Quadrant #4 **Deep-Rooted Kinship** Hubs and other writing communities like Prolific Writers Life

This final category includes writing communities that are long-term deep hubs, such as Prolific Writers Life. They're the rare groups that offer deep-rooted kinship. These writing communities have the following attributes:

- **Long-term Collaboration:** You write with people over a long period, building mutual respect and trust as you continue to collaborate and grow together.

- **Expert Guidance:** You receive support and mentorship from experienced authors and writing industry experts who are dedicated to helping you succeed in your writing projects.

- **Broad Network:** The community connects you with a broad range of experts across the writing industry, offering valuable insights and opportunities.

- **Supportive Home Base:** You have a reliable group of peers to report back to after festivals, conferences, and retreats, who are genuinely interested in your experiences and progress.

- **Mutual Learning:** Communication flows both ways, allowing members to learn from experts and for experts to gain insights from the community.

- **Lifelong Friendships:** You form lasting friendships that contribute to your ongoing personal and professional growth as a writer.

- **Autonomy in Projects:** There are no mandatory assignments; you bring your own projects, fostering a sense of ownership and self-direction.

- **Open Membership:** New members are always welcome, ensuring a continuously evolving and dynamic community.

- **Personal Growth:** The community supports your writing and overall personal development, encouraging you to evolve as a writer and an individual.

- **Collaborative Opportunities:** There are frequent opportunities for collaborative projects, co-writing, and sharing resources, enhancing your creative output.

- **Feedback and Reflection:** The environment encourages constructive feedback and reflection, helping you refine your work and approach in a supportive setting.

- **Resource Sharing:** Members have access to shared resources, tools, and knowledge that benefit their writing process and professional growth.

In his 2008 book *Outliers*, Malcolm Gladwell shared that "ten thousand hours is the magic number of greatness." For those who are passionate about writing and aiming for success, I wanted to create a space where they could gather with fellow lifelong learners. Here, they can share in those ten thousand hours of learning, making the journey more efficient and enriching through the power of community. And, most importantly, they can have fun doing it.

After acquiring six college degrees and teaching as a professor, there's one thing I'm sure about when it comes to learning: It's best done hands-on with real-life projects. Institutional learning often lacks realism and passion, resulting in uninspired work that's quickly abandoned. Learners who engage in real-life projects gain a significant advantage, seeing tangible outcomes from their efforts.

This is not a dress rehearsal. You are center stage in your own life. If you want to grow as a writer, the best way to do it is to write about things that spark your interest and give you the chance to express your core values and life purpose.

I started Prolific Writers Life because I was looking for a place to connect regularly with authors and experts in the writing industry. I was looking for a community that offered expert-led events and continuous online engagement, accessible from anywhere, and that accommodated our RV lifestyle, opening up opportunities to work with people not only in the US but also from other countries. At Prolific Writers Life, there's no limit to the number of experts you can meet.

There's no limit to how many different workshops you can take and how many daily work sessions you can attend. You can go as deep as you want in your learning. You have a group of peers who become virtual colleagues in your writing life.

You can create lifelong friendships, not only with authors but also with writing industry experts. You see them frequently over a long period. It's a coworking space where you get guidance from people you trust, people who have been vetted by the community. Prolific Writers Life is founded on a culture of passionate individuals dedicated to helping fellow writers. If someone takes advantage of a fellow member, word quickly spreads through the community. And they tend to expel themselves from the community because they simply don't fit in. Prolific Writers Life offers members the opportunity to build deep-rooted connections that can lead to lifelong friendships. It's the home you come back to after participating in other literary events.

The Unique Role of a Writing Community

As writers, we're aware of the power of words. They evoke life, stir emotions, and spur people into action. This is what draws us to the page–a deep need to express ideas, capture meaning, and communicate something that matters. The support and camaraderie in a writing community filled with friends can't be replicated at a fleeting writing conference or retreat. Our writing projects unfold day by day, making a writing community the optimal space to learn, grow, and share the journey with fellow writers. Having friends who comprehend the challenges and triumphs of investing time and effort into our writing lives is priceless. You simply can't find this outside of a writing community.

A Quadrant #4 writing community is like Noah's Ark when it was at capacity, teeming with life forces — each one encapsulated in fur, feathers, or scales — acting out their unique superpowers and vulnerabilities. Every living creature plays an essential role in maintaining a robust and balanced ecosystem. Similarly, a Quadrant #4 writing community thrives with a wide range of individuals, each bringing their unique life experiences and genres, sharing stories, guidance, and support. This community, much like a modern-day Noah's Ark, is not just filled with one type of energy but with a broad range, like zebras, giraffes, ducks, bees, and tortoises, all representing different levels of energy, perspectives, and strengths. This range is crucial to creating a dynamic, spirited, and balanced writing ecosystem where everyone can flourish.

In such a writing community, we share tips, encourage each other, and cheer each other on when someone has a book launch. We engage with each other regularly. We're involved in each other's writing lives because we work together as colleagues. We're a family of writers. It's so nice to have others who understand your challenges and what you must overcome to invest that time and effort into your writing life. Fellow writers may not have experienced the exact situations, but their collective wisdom can help you overcome inevitable obstacles.

Before I started Prolific Writers Life, my writing life was fragmented. Over the years, I have started writers' groups, participated in those led by others, and attended writing conferences, book festivals, and all sorts of events for writers. I went to one group on Thursday evenings and another on Friday afternoons. I also attended state-run writing group meetings once a month. For the most part, the people in these various groups didn't know each other, and it all felt disconnected. Throughout my adult life, I've been part of different writing communities—sporadic gatherings, occasional meetings, or monthly sessions of local groups, wherever I lived at the time. I joined critique groups, state groups, and local groups, and while they all offered ways to meet with other writers, the experience was often unpredictable. I never knew who would show up or how helpful any given meeting might be. After years of countless disconnected group experiences, I realized that having a sense of community would tie everything together. Meeting once a week or less frequently simply wasn't enough for the connection and consistency I craved as a writer.

After years of conforming to the status quo, I realized that having one writing community led by various experts in the writing industry was essential to pulling everything together. Prolific Writers Life has been my passion project since I began developing the idea in 2018. I wholeheartedly believe that Prolific Writers Life will enrich your writing life, unlike anything else you've ever experienced as a writer.

The Impact of a Daily Writing Community

When launching Prolific Writers Life, my vision was to create a space for daily interactions with fellow writers. With activities scheduled nearly every day of the week, this rhythm has become part of my daily routine. It serves as a consistent reminder that my writing matters and that the collaboration with fellow members strengthens not only my work but also the work of everyone involved.

Being part of a writing community encourages me to explore other writing strategies and genres, such as poetry or blogging. Being around fellow writers has had a huge positive impact on me as a writer in my daily writing life.

As the founder of Prolific Writers Life, I am first and foremost another writer within the community. Leading isn't my primary goal; it's about creating a space where writers can consistently connect with one another. Our experts offer workshops and work sessions throughout the week, creating an environment where we can share our journeys, learn from one another, and finish our books.

Community Building Online: Prolific Writers Life

I started Prolific Writers Life because I was tired of sitting at hierarchical rectangular tables, answering to the guy at the head of the table. I was eager to work with fellow creatives at round tables. As an interior design major, I learned how architecture and furniture shape the way we interact with people. I prefer round tables where people can talk as peers. The point of a writing community is for you to grow in knowledge, strength, and wisdom and be empowered to make decisions about your writing life. The Prolific Writers Life logo is a circle for a reason. I believe everyone has talent and wisdom to bring to the table.

A writing community thrives when it includes writers from different cultures, backgrounds, occupations, life experiences, and genres. While it's enriching to immerse yourself in a genre-based community like sci-fi, the real magic happens in a broader community. Here, you're surrounded by writers with a wide range of "superpowers" — unique ways their minds spark ideas. This cross-pollination fosters creativity, keeps us sharp, and sparks fresh perspectives. Just as Noah's Ark was a microcosm of life's variety, a varied writing community nurtures and grows our creative superpowers exponentially.

So, what do people do in a writing community that offers deep-rooted kinship? Some of the activities are similar to those found in writing festivals, associations, or conferences, but you also have the opportunity to build long-term relationships with people who are familiar with your goals.

Many tech tools divide our attention and our tasks, but Prolific Writers Life leverages technology to bring writers together in live, virtual conversations so you can keep your vision at the forefront of your mind. If your writing tasks are scattered, your writing life will feel disjointed. You can't count on software applications, tutorial videos, and writing forums to succeed at writing a bestselling book.

People who care about you and your writing goals can help you reach them. Virtual gatherings with fellow writers from here, there, and everywhere are lifelines. Connecting with fellow writers reminds me that my writing matters. Being part of a virtual writing community keeps writing at the forefront of my daily life, pushing me to grow and learn. It encourages me to explore various writing styles and genre techniques and go beyond my comfort zone. It's what propelled me to finish this book. After being part of a virtual writing community for the past several years, I can't imagine life without it.

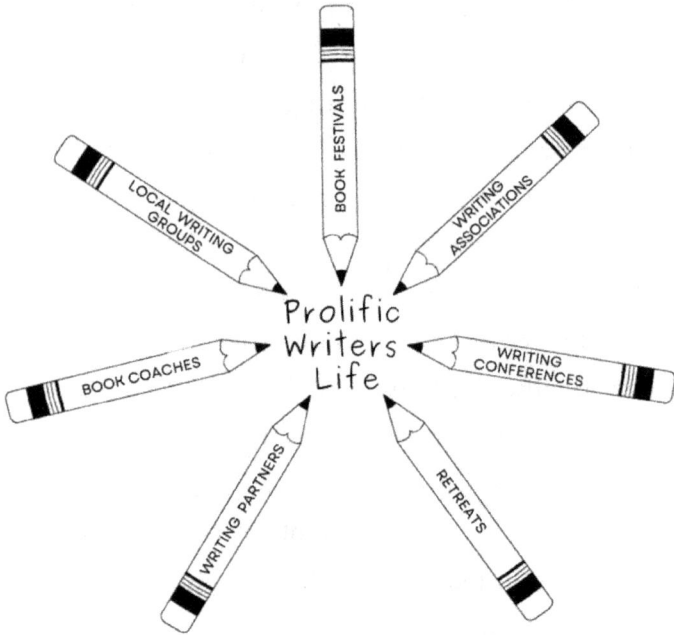

The Prolific Writers Life diagram showing: BOOK FESTIVALS, WRITING ASSOCIATIONS, LOCAL WRITING GROUPS, BOOK COACHES, WRITING CONFERENCES, WRITING PARTNERS, RETREATS

Explore and Flourish: The Ever-Expanding Writing Community

Exploring different writing groups, conferences, and associations is important. Find the ones that resonate with your goals and needs, and remain open to allowing them to help you flourish as a writer.

When you're navigating different writing groups, conferences, and associations, it's crucial to understand the varying levels of connection and support they can offer. From fleeting encounters at book festivals and conferences to short-term deep bonds formed in writing retreats or with beta readers, each category brings unique benefits and challenges. Long-term connections in local writing groups, associations, and critique groups offer enduring support, but also come with potential limitations.

I encourage you to participate in a variety of writing communities and gatherings based on your current needs and interests. And I urge you to participate in a cross-genre writing community that gives you a chance to build long-term, deep-rooted relationships with fellow writers, authors, and experts in the industry. The people who show up in such writing communities want to build relationships and learn from those they meet. Simply put, people who join writing groups are much more likely to be committed to lifelong learning. They recognize the value of learning from one another. They actively try out new strategies and grow their skill set.

Prolific Writers Life is my heart's project, born from a desire to create an uplifting community that's always there for you. A community that provides deep-rooted kinship represents an ideal co-working space. Hubs like Prolific Writers Life foster an environment where writers of all levels connect as peers, receive guidance from industry experts, and cultivate lasting friendships. This hub offers a continuous, hands-on learning experience, ensuring writers not only survive but thrive in their journey. With a team of experts committed to member success, Prolific Writers Life stands as a testament to the power of a writing community dedicated to writers' lifelong growth and success.

We come together to support each other as writers, accepting each other in a spirit of peace and unconditional love regardless of our faith, political beliefs, country of origin, race or ethnicity, cultural practices, education level, lifestyle choices, age, economic status and any other factors that could be divisive among people. We honor our differences and various backgrounds as the very strength of our connection as writers.

CHAPTER 9

Gather. Write. Share. Repeat.

As a member of Prolific Writers Life, I love knowing that I can wake up any morning and find something on the calendar almost every day of the week. It's such a great feeling to touch base with fellow writers, authors, and industry experts while keeping my focus on writing. At the time of this writing, we are currently celebrating our fifth anniversary with Prolific Writers Life, and I can honestly say that the past five years of my writing life have been so much more enjoyable and fulfilling than any of the years before. What I absolutely love is the gathering, the writing, the sharing, and having this consistent, supportive community always there for me — it makes writing so much more fun!

Writing is a journey, a continuous cycle of gathering, writing, and sharing. This process is the core of your work, interweaving with your life as you collect information and experiences, write about them, and then share your stories with readers.

Gathering is essential to your writing process. Without life experiences and interactions, what would you write about? Solitude lets you explore your inner thoughts, but engaging with the world provides the raw material for your stories. These interactions are the fruits you pick from your life, and the ingredients you incorporate into your writing.

This cycle of gathering, writing, and sharing sustains your creativity at every stage. Gathering enriches your ideas, writing refines them, and sharing brings them to life for your readers. While writing often involves solitude, connecting with a supportive community of fellow writers for feedback and encouragement is crucial. By repeating this cycle, you keep your creative spark alive and ensure ongoing growth as a writer.

Gather

Writers are, by nature, gatherers. We gather stories, ideas, and facts and weave them into our work. This instinct extends beyond information; we also gather with each other and our readers. We observe people, and their character traits often appear in our books.

Writing is an act of reflection and creation, drawing from our life experiences, observations, and research. This gathering provides the raw materials we need to construct our books.

Writers seek the company of fellow writers and readers to form connections that offer support, inspiration, and a shared sense of purpose. Writing groups, book festivals, and conferences provide spaces for learning and growth. Engaging with writers and industry experts exposes us to new perspectives and possibilities, enhancing our work in unexpected ways.

Gathering Stories, Ideas, and Facts

Writers have a natural inclination to collect ideas. We gather stories, facts, and character traits from our experiences, observations, and research. We compile notes about the characters in our lives and use words as our medium to piece together elements. This is a fundamental aspect of a writer's life. We reflect on our experiences, pulling stories from them, and puzzling them together into paragraphs and chapters. Eventually, we organize the right mix of stories, ideas, and facts to create our books. The gathering of information and ideas serves as the foundation for constructing our work.

Gathering With Fellow Writers and Readers

Writers come together for many reasons, but above all, they gather to connect with individuals who share their values: an appreciation for the written word, a passion for storytelling, and a commitment to finishing their books.

When I was close to finishing this book, I had a conversation with Rod Sanford during one of his Words Count writing sessions. I expressed my concern about constantly finding ways to improve the book. Rod reminded me that, like movies, books need to be released even though they could always be further refined. This is why authors put out second or third editions — to update and improve them over time. His advice was to release the book without overworking it. This is one of the significant benefits of being a member of a writing community — gaining new perspectives and valuable encouragement from fellow writers.

Engaging with fellow writers offers a multitude of benefits. Whether through writers' conferences, accountability partnerships, or writing groups, participating in a broader writing community provides opportunities for learning, growth, and personal development. Building relationships with writers from various genres, age groups, cultures, and professions exposes you to a wealth of perspectives and possibilities you may not have previously considered. Investing time in a writing community allows you to cultivate deep connections with individuals who genuinely care about your progress. Fellow writers offer valuable guidance and support as you navigate your writing journey. Writing a book is a big project, and one you do not need to do on your own.

And guess what? In a community filled with comrades, writers become devoted to fellow writers and their projects as well. As connections transition into friendship, writers recognize the need to hold each other accountable to their writing goals and dreams. You were called to write a book, but you were not meant to go through this mysterious maze on your own. As a writer, one of the most important things you need is a community of fellow writers and experts who are eager to help you succeed.

Immersing yourself in a community with both writers and writing industry experts opens up the opportunity for you to address a wide range of topics essential to your development as a writer—from establishing productive habits to overcoming obstacles like perfectionism or lack of focus. Often, these challenges go unrecognized until you find yourself embraced by a supportive network, where you realize the transformative power of community engagement. Once you experience it, you will likely find it difficult to return to the solitary path of writing alone, where it's easy to wander aimlessly for many months or even years. Where two or more writers are gathered, much can be accomplished. Incidentally, you can be uplifted by the support of fellow writers who never read your book.

Connecting With Readers

It's essential for writers to engage with their readers and potential audience members. Personal interaction with fans is one of the best ways to build lasting connections with people who eagerly await your next book. Whether you meet in person or virtually, these interactions show your gratitude and help strengthen the bond between you and your readers. Connecting with your audience is an important element in building engaged readers.

Literary Rituals & Gatherings

Like routines, rituals are a series of activities that you perform in sequence. But rituals often include a deeper sense of purpose or intention. They come laced with tradition, practices, and unwritten rules. Here are a few examples of rituals in the literary world:

- Book Launch: Introduce your new book to readers by doing a book reading and book signing. It's appropriate to socialize with visitors, but not okay to pressure them to sign up for your email list.

- Book Clubs: Come prepared to share your thoughts and ask questions, but don't interrupt others or berate them if they don't agree with your interpretation of the book.

- Manuscript Submissions: Submit your book proposal or manuscript to agents who are seeking new clients with books like yours. Be sure to follow their submission guidelines. If not, you're wasting your time and theirs.

- Literary Award Ceremonies: Dress appropriately for the occasion and show appreciation for the organizers and sponsors. Don't be late, tell coarse jokes, or drink too much alcohol.

- Writing Conferences: It's advantageous to bring business cards and promotional materials to share with others, but inappropriate to firehose people with all the details of your book, or to stalk agents or editors.

- Festival Booths: Display your books prominently and be prepared to engage with attendees and ask them to sign up for your mailing list, but don't oversell your book or make false claims, and don't break any festival rules, such as using a megaphone to draw people to your booth.

If you're a newbie author, you may not be familiar with the many ceremonies and taboos in the literary world. You can benefit tremendously by learning from seasoned authors and experts. However, don't be intimidated by such authorities, especially those with big egos who want to tell you how things are done. As a newbie, you're well-positioned to bring fresh ideas to stale traditional rituals. The publishing world has undergone big changes in the past few decades, and things continue to evolve. Just because your local book festival has been doing things a certain way for years, for example, doesn't mean it still makes sense to continue doing things the same way. Delve into different writing communities and get involved. As long as you have a positive outlook, Karma has a way of returning your volunteer time and good deeds in big measure.

In her book *The Art of Gathering*, Priya Parker distinguishes between a gathering "category" and a gathering "purpose." A networking event, a volunteer training, or a book club meeting is a "category" without a stated purpose. She suggests that saying you will start a book club because you want to read books together is "circular logic." She urges participants to go deeper into the purpose of gathering and ask "why," not just once, but repeatedly, until they get to a meaningful and transformative purpose for a gathering. Book clubs can serve many purposes. Here are just a few examples of possible core aims:

- Support locals by encouraging book club members to meet at and purchase their books by local authors from a particular local indie bookstore café.
- Read books with storylines about parenting to build relationships between moms in a neighborhood so they can support each other's parenting journeys.
- Promote cultural awareness and appreciation by reading books written by authors from other countries; translated books are welcome.

If you've ever been a book club member, were you clear on its purpose? Without a stated purpose, any group risks falling apart when members have scattered expectations.

The same holds true for writing groups — it's helpful to understand the purpose of the group before you get involved. The next time you consider participating in a literary event, ask questions. Regardless of where you are in your writing journey, you'll be better off if you understand the purpose of the gathering. Pay attention. Ask questions. Learn and grow.

Even if you consider yourself a veteran author who's in the know, it's beneficial to change the status quo and ramp up your creativity when preparing for an upcoming event. Be bold. Try something new. Writing communities are an ideal place to collaborate and exchange ideas before heading off to your next literary event.

Write

Writing in Solitude

You're drawn to writing because you enjoy exploring your thoughts and ideas free from the influence of others. Escaping to a quiet place is a strong draw for many writers. There are and always will be times when you seek solitude to write a first draft or revise a manuscript. Nevertheless, you can benefit tremendously by balancing your time in solitude and mingling with fellow writers. You need validation for your progress, and you need readers. Having a community where you can bounce ideas around provides inspiration to keep going.

Write Now: The Best Strategy to Finish Your Book

When it comes to writing your book, there's no better day than today. You can't change what you did yesterday, and you can't predict what might happen tomorrow. So, write today. This is the best plan of action to take to finish your book.

Many books, blogs, podcasts, and magazine articles for writers address the topic of time management. I saved this topic for later in the book because I believe the time issue takes care of itself if you work on the elements of your writing life in the right order. Consider the following questions:

- Do you have a compelling reason for writing your book (see Chapter 1)?
- Do you connect with fellow writers and authors on a regular basis to share your writing life (see Chapter 2)?

- Do you trust that your desire to write this book means you're ready to begin (see Chapter 3)?

- Are you taking steps to improve your writing habits and routines (see Chapter 4)?

- Have you designed a fool-proof writing system that works for you, one you thoroughly enjoy (see Chapter 5)?

- Do you understand the power of maintaining momentum on your book (see Chapter 6)?

- Do you have strategies to handle disappointments, surprises, distractions, interruptions, and setbacks? (Chapter 7)

- Are you a member of a supportive writing community that provides opportunities to learn from authors and experts in the industry (see Chapter 8)?

- Are you willing to admit to yourself that you always find time to do the things that are most appealing to you (Chapter 9)?

If you progress in each of these areas, you will find the time and energy to write your book. As you develop your writing practice, you will be able to feel good about what you accomplished as you look back on each day.

Writing in Community

Writing work sessions are ideal for writers embarking on a journey filled with mysteries and questions. New writers can benefit from writing alongside seasoned authors, learning about the writing process and discovering what works best for them. There isn't one way to write a book; there are countless approaches to producing a manuscript and eventually a published book.

Consider a construction site for a large building, where workers use scaffolding to access various heights. Scaffolding, often independent from the building but attached as it rises, elevates workers to where they need to be. Similarly, a writing community serves as scaffolding for your book. The community elevates you at different stages of your writing process, offering new perspectives and support so you can build and layer your words until they're ready to stand on their own.

Joining a writing community is essential. The community provides regular interaction with fellow writers who help you hone your system and encourage you as you construct your book. These supportive writers form the strongest part of your scaffolding.

Writing independently is like using a ladder to construct a skyscraper when you really need a crane.

For small projects, like blog posts or articles, a ladder (a few friends) might suffice. But for a book, you'll benefit more from scaffolding and a crane (larger writing communities) with bigger ideas and teams. Collaboration and feedback strengthen you as a writer and enhance your skills.

Share

Within a writing community, knowledge flows freely. We learn from each other's experiences, gaining insights into writing techniques, marketing strategies, and the publishing world. It's a melting pot of wisdom where seasoned authors guide newcomers, making the writing journey more accessible and rewarding for everyone.

I love to host and participate in writing workshops, panel discussions, and writing podcasts, but nothing beats a friendly conversation with writing peers who have off-the-cuff suggestions at just the right time when you need them. When you share your writing life with fellow writers, you will stretch and grow in ways you never imagined. And you will be much better informed than writers who work independently.

What do writers do when they gather? They share their stories — the ones they're writing and the stories of how they're managing their writing life. These layers of storytelling are all crucial to succeeding as a writer.

Reading about everything involved in finishing your book might feel overwhelming, but it becomes a fun and rewarding challenge with ongoing support from fellow writers. Within the community, you'll hear both success stories and cautionary tales. Whether or not things went well, you learn from these experiences, making it worthwhile to show up.

Even if you're content with your writing life, I encourage you to get involved with a writing community. You don't know what you're missing. Until you're fully engaged, you won't realize how much more fulfilling your writing life could be. If you've made it this far into the book and aren't part of a writing community, you likely sense my nudge to join one as soon as possible.

Navigating the Publishing Maze

Just because you've thought about writing a book doesn't mean you've fully considered what it means to be an author. You might have a great idea for a book and dive right into writing. But after a few years of writing and reworking your manuscript, you could find yourself feeling stuck or going in circles. Maybe you haven't thought much about how you'd publish or market your book. Publishing a book is a lot like starting a business — it involves more than just writing. But don't worry, with some planning and support, you can navigate the process and share your work with the world.

Navigating your way through publishing your first book is like trying to find your way out of a maze with many turns and trap doors. Deciding whether to self-publish, go hybrid, or pursue traditional houses is only the first step. Within each of these publishing routes, there are more options to consider. It's common to feel overwhelmed with all the possibilities.

The good news is that you don't have to stay lost in this maze. Seek advice from a writing community where you can learn from the experiences of authors and industry experts. With their help and guidance, you'll be much better equipped to choose a publishing path that's right for you. When you're part of a writing community, you'll hear personal stories from fellow members, get valuable insights into the industry, and learn about various publishing options to make an informed decision about what makes sense for your book.

Over the years, I've met many people who have self-published their books, only to make mistakes that could have been easily avoided with active involvement in a writing community. Some common errors include not having a title on the spine, regretting not getting their own ISBN, misspellings in the blurb on the back, formatting issues that confuse readers, and poor font choices on the book cover that make it hard to read. Being part of a writing community can raise awareness about these critical details, ensuring that your final book is the best it can be.

Once you begin your publishing journey, remember that publishers handle many tasks for you, such as book editing, book formatting, and cover design. Most, however, do not help to market your book beyond your book launch. Once your book is released, it's all on you. Align your expectations with the reality of industry standards and avoid unnecessary shock. The publisher will help you birth your baby (your book), but they're not going home with you to help you raise it in the world. This is where a writing community is even more valuable. Talk to authors, publishers, and book marketing experts to come up with the best publishing and marketing strategy for your book.

Sharing Your Words

The whole point of writing, for the most part, is sharing what you've written. This is the most impactful aspect of being a writer — exposing your ideas. This can be a daunting task for some writers. Whether you're sharing a journal entry, a blog post, or quotes on social media, starting small helps you become comfortable sharing larger volumes of your work with people you've never met. Other ways to do this include participating in critique groups or attending open mic events. These can be valuable experiences for you and help you to prepare for future book readings.

Sharing your written words is the ideal way to connect with readers and grow a following. It can provide a huge sense of fulfillment with your work as you see other people showing up and appreciating your work.

One of the superpowers of a book lies in its ability to endure beyond the lifetime of you, the author. Writing allows us to capture moments of triumph and tragedy, weaving them into stories that inspire and connect with readers in present and future generations. Books are a force for change, entertainment, and empathy that can shape lives long after we, the writers, are gone. Writing and publishing a book is one of the greatest gifts you can leave behind.

Your Virtual Amphitheater

I'm intrigued by amphitheaters, especially ones that are outdoors. I love the circular design. It creates an energy flow that encircles the stands and continues around the stage. Imagine a stone amphitheater built into the side of a sloping hill. It's summertime. The amphitheater is surrounded by tall trees, providing just the right amount of shade to stay cool on this sunny day. Now, imagine that you're participating in an event here today. You're one of the speakers. You will read a passage from your book and talk about what inspired you to write the book. Your fans are eager to hear your talk.

The amphitheater provides a terrific way to visualize your audience. If you prefer, your amphitheater can be near a beach or wherever you'd like. Now, imagine your fans showing up to hear what you have to say. You're standing center-stage. How many people do you envision? Are you happy with the number of people showing up? Do you want to attract more?

What's nice about an outdoor amphitheater is that Mother Nature surrounds you, so it's nearly impossible to feel alone or like a failure.

Your readers are your audience, and your writing community is part of your behind-the-scenes support team. Whether writing a blog post or doing a podcast interview, I imagine my audience at the amphitheater with me. They come freely, and they're free to leave at any time. My job as a writer is to entertain, teach, and encourage them so that they'll want to come back the next time I have something to share.

Your writing platform is like an amphitheater, the stage from which you share your message with your audience, inviting them into your world and leaving them craving more. Your writing community is there to encourage you to share your stories with passion, purpose, and unwavering enthusiasm. Set the stage. The world is eagerly awaiting your performance.

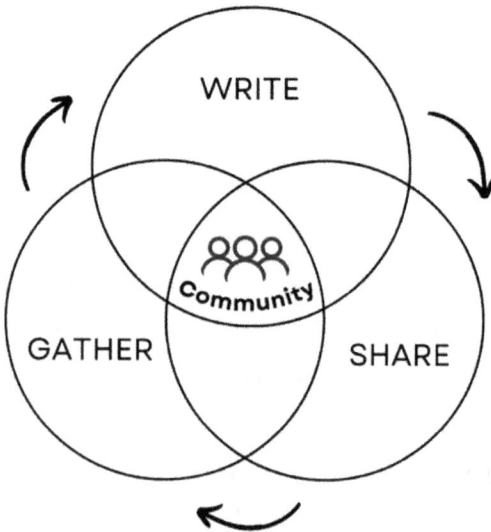

Repeat the Process: Gather, Write, Share

The writer's journey is a repetitive cycle of gathering, writing, and sharing. It's important to find joy in each phase. It's worth your time to determine where you find satisfaction in each aspect. If you spend 80% or more of your time doing what you most love to do, then you're much more likely to continue doing it. If you love going on podcasts to talk about your book (sharing), that's what you should be doing. If you don't like doing social media (sharing), then don't spend your time there. Finding satisfaction in gathering, writing, and sharing enhances your writing journey.

Being part of various writing communities over the years, especially Prolific Writers Life, has been a transformative experience for me. Constant interactions, sharing tips and encouragement, and recognizing each other's successes create an atmosphere of genuine support. It's a place where friends understand the challenges and triumphs of the writing process.

During the gathering stage, many writers love meeting authors and experts and learning from them. Whether you enjoy learning, meeting people, researching, or interviewing experts, find the pathway that brings you joy in gathering ideas.

The writing process includes all sorts of things from drafting to revising and other promotional efforts, and then finally, sharing — offering your work to the world through various means.

To maximize your experience through this cycle, joining a supportive writing community should be a top priority. This can help you to make your journey much more fun, and you're much more likely to be pleased with the outcome of your book.

There's no reason ever to feel lonely or stuck or frustrated. When you're an active member of a writing community, the whole process becomes much more enjoyable. You can finish your book and have fun doing it.

Remember the title of this book? *Finish Your Book: Plug into the Power of a Writing Community and Get it Done.* Joining a writing community won't do you much good unless you participate. It's like signing up for a gym membership — you won't see results unless you actually show up and move with the music.

Your Journey is Just Beginning...

I love how my dear friend, Keiko O'Leary, ended her book, *Your Writing Matters*. The last chapter is entitled "Not the End." In this chapter, she states, "You'll never be done learning, and you can't do everything on your own. We need other people. We need community, both in person and in text...Let's keep learning and supporting each other. Let's keep writing. This is not the end" (p. 146).

Finish Your Book is more than just a guide–it's an invitation. As Keiko reminds us, learning and growth don't end here. Now is the time to connect with others who understand the challenges and joys of writing, to share your progress, and to keep moving forward together. Come be part of Prolific Writers Life, where the camaraderie and shared experience make the writing journey more rewarding and fulfilling.

CHAPTER 10

Join a Writing Community

Imagine walking alone in a bustling foreign city where you don't speak the local language. I've had this experience many times. It can be both exhilarating and exhausting at the same time. This is what it's like when you're a writer without a writing community. You see things that look familiar, but you're unsure how to communicate or get around. If you're serious about your writing life, it's important to immerse yourself in a writing community. What worked a couple of years ago can be as obsolete as a typewriter or floppy drive today.

By now, you should be feeling the excitement and possibilities that a writing community can bring to your life. There's absolutely no need for you to go on this writing journey alone. In fact, there are countless reasons why you should be part of a supportive community of writers. Take the leap and join Prolific Writers Life today.

Even if you're not quite ready to embark on your next book or project, that's okay. There's something extraordinary about being surrounded by like-minded individuals who share your passion for writing, whether books, blogs, poetry, chapbooks, or journaling. In our virtual writing community, you'll find the inspiration and motivation to take that next step, no matter where you are in your writing journey.

As the founder of Prolific Writers Life, I've witnessed the incredible transformations that writers undergo once they become part of our community. It's amazing to see how their writing lives flourish, and their confidence soars as they discover they have a dedicated support team cheering them on. You deserve a space where you're surrounded by unconditional love and support.

So, my dear friend, I wholeheartedly invite you to check out Prolific Writers Life. Here, you'll meet fantastic fellow writers and authors and connect with industry experts who will guide you on your unique path to success.

Don't wait any longer; now is the time to join us at Prolific Writers Life. Let's share the writing journey. Head over to prolificwriters.life/finish-your-book and become a member of our incredible community today. I can't wait to welcome you. Together, we'll finish our books and create the writing life of our dreams!

Praise for Prolific Writers Life from Our Members

"I never would have finished my book without Prolific Writers Life."

Keiko O'Leary
Author, Poet Laureate,
Small Press Co-Founder

"Through sharing, you motivate the other person. The next thing you know, by helping somebody else, you've helped yourself."

Todd Gardner
Graphic Designer, Artist, Writer

"Prolific Writers Life is a merging of brilliant minds. I had this dream ruminating in my head of what I wanted...Now it's here; it's becoming a manuscript."

Karen Lorraine Collado
Writer, Research Assistant,
Working on a Bachelor's Degree

"I have found a whole new group of literary friends who have also proven to be a fantastic resource for learning about every aspect of the modern business of writing, from problem-solving your way through a first draft all the way through a full publication process."

David Hern
Actor, Award Winning Author,
Screenwriter, Playwright

"To be a writer is a passionate pursuit of who we are. To be part of a writing community who cheer you on every step of the way, is pure magic. That is how we tell our stories and finish our books. Thank you, Lorraine, for your infinite support, and to Prolific Writers Life — It certainly saved mine!"

Colleen Grace Clabby
Intuitive Spiritual Counselor, Writer

"Prolific Writers Life is a little bit like my literary comfort food. It's a really nice ratio of work to connection. You don't get bored; you get as much done as you want and set your own goals."

Ryan Christopher Hicks
Travel Writer and Audiobook Expert

"It's useful to have events on the calendar, times of dedicated concentration, where you are expected to log on and be part of this writing process."

Matthew Gollub
Children's Book Author, Presenter, Publisher

"Writing is a solitary practice, and you can't change that, but you can make it easier by writing together with other people. The diversity in experience levels — some attendees are writing their first pieces while others have been writing for decades — leads to amazing conversations. We share tips, commiserate over challenges, and celebrate wins together, big or small."

Liza Olmsted
Publisher, Editor, Writer

"Being a member of Prolific Writers Life, having that accountability and having the group to work with really helped me get into the mood of writing and get going."

Lyndley Fehr
Certified Intuitive Coach,
Frequency Healing Practitioner, Author

Acknowledgments

I want to express my heartfelt appreciation to every member of Prolific Writers Life. Your participation and collaboration have made this book possible and deeply fulfilling. Writing can often feel isolating, but sharing this journey with each of you has made it more enjoyable and filled with endless insights for this book and many more to come. Thank you for being part of this shared mission and for making Prolific Writers Life a place where writers finish their books!

I extend my gratitude to the many writers who have been part of this book-writing journey. I want to acknowledge a few of the Prolific Writers Life members who shared countless hours with me in Words Count writing sessions during this experience: Colleen Grace Clabby, David Hern, Karen Lorraine Collado, Lyndley Fehr, Lisa Kron, Leilani Jeffries, Liza Olmsted, Matthew Gollub, Todd Gardner, and Rod Sanford. In particular, I would like to thank some of the following founding members who are also depicted on the front cover of this book: Bob Haataia, Linton McClain, Keiko O'Leary, Maya Carlyle, Paula Wagner, and Ryan Hicks.

I want to express sincere gratitude to Renée Chio, the illustrator of my book cover. I had been stuck envisioning the design until I spoke with Renée. She immediately understood my vision and created an illustration that far exceeded my expectations. I am deeply grateful for her creative talent and artistry.

Special thanks to the beta readers who provided insightful feedback on my book: Linton McClain, Colleen Grace Clabby, Paula Wagner, Ryan Hicks, Keiko O'Leary, David Hern, Amanda Haataia, and Ivan Farber.

I'm deeply grateful to my editor, Tanya Brockett, whose talent and dedication have been essential in shaping this book. Her sharp eye and thoughtful feedback helped make this manuscript the best it could be.

I am also profoundly thankful for the Prolific Writers Life pioneers and the supporters who helped me shape this community into what it is today. The journey began at A Work of Heart Studio in San Jose, California, where Andrea Chebeleu facilitated *Creative Entrepreneur Power Hour* gatherings. During these sessions, I developed the initial ideas for Prolific Writers Life, refining my vision for the community I wanted to create. Among those instrumental in the early days were

Keiko O'Leary and Mary Pascal, our very first community member. Today, both are accomplished authors. Keiko, in particular, has been a steadfast supporter, serving on the advisory board, as a community member, and as an expert, offering guidance and encouragement to our members.

I would also like to thank Susan Cameron, president of Rough Writers Toastmasters, and the many members of Rough Writers who have provided consistent support and encouragement throughout this journey. The *Silent Writing* sessions, *Writer Spotlight & Feedback Hour* sessions, and thoughtful discussions have been instrumental in refining my writing.

Additionally, I want to acknowledge our marketing team, who has been instrumental in helping us grow the Prolific Writers Life community. Dinara Jayakody has expanded our community's reach through newsletters, digital images, and social media shares about our members, events, and products. Krishan Kanishka has supported our marketing and social media efforts through impactful testimonial videos and other creative content.

I also want to thank my aunt, Gail Kandor, who was like a second mother to me—a wise and uplifting guide, especially during my college years. She instilled in me the understanding that the only way to succeed is to follow your heart, and she gave me the assurance I needed to pursue a career centered on writing. Though she has moved on from this earthly life, I still feel her presence, affirming my path and reminding me of who I am. I remember her dearly as someone who always had a book in her hand during our late-night conversations and who often drifted off while reading on the couch — an avid reader and true lover of the written word.

Finally, I want to extend my gratitude to the too-many-to-name teachers, professors, mentors, writers, authors, and industry experts who have coached, taught, and encouraged me over the years. Your insights and support have been invaluable in shaping my writing journey.

My deepest thanks go to my husband, Bob Haataia. Without his unwavering support and technical expertise, Prolific Writers Life would never have come to fruition. His dedication turned my vision of a virtual writing community into reality. His exceptional technical skills, along with his ability to solve complex problems, never cease to amaze me.

Acknowledgments

Thank you to my beloved cats, Namaste and Dharma, for keeping me company through countless hours of writing—whether in my office, on the patio, or in our RV. Their playful energy, calming presence, and instinctual meows always seem to come at just the right moment, reminding me when it's time for a break. I'm endlessly grateful for their unconditional love, soft purrs, and gentle reminders to pause. They've been my quiet companions every step of the way.

I humbly acknowledge divine guidance throughout the writing of this book and in the creation of Prolific Writers Life—a community where writers can experience the same sense of love and support that has nurtured me throughout my journey. I'm grateful for the opportunity to live my calling as a writer while helping others feel connected, inspired, and encouraged along their own creative paths.

May the positive karma you all have shared with me return to you in abundance and ripple outward, bringing love and peace to our extended family of writers for many years to come.

About the Author

Dr. Lorraine Haataia is a devoted supporter of writers, providing them with the community, resources, and connections they need to thrive. As the Founder of Prolific Writers Life, she launched the platform in 2020 to help writers connect with live experts through workshops and collaborative sessions. Lorraine holds six degrees, including a PhD achieved before age 35. She has worked in various fields, from content marketing and grant evaluation to ISO 9001 and 14001 documentation and continuous improvement. She has also served as a professor at several universities and colleges in the U.S. and France, where she absolutely loved teaching and sharing her passion for writing.

Lorraine has earned recognition for her work, including the Distinguished Toastmasters Award, and has shared her insights on podcasts, television, and both TEDx and stand-up comedy stages. Her writing has been published internationally, shaped by her experiences living in the U.S., France, and China, as well as her extensive travel to dozens of countries. Currently based in Arizona, Lorraine, along with her techie husband, Bob, and their two cats, Namaste and Dharma, roam the U.S. in their Leisure Travel Van, exploring new vistas and inspiring fellow writers along the way.

www.ingramcontent.com/pod-product-compliance
Lightning Source LLC
Chambersburg PA
CBHW051416090426
42737CB00014B/2697